COTTON-PATCH
SCHOOLHOUSE

COTTON-PATCH SCHOOLHOUSE

Susie Powers Tompkins
With Illustrations by the Author

THE UNIVERSITY OF ALABAMA PRESS
Tuscaloosa and London

Library of Congress Cataloging-in-Publication Data

Tompkins, Susie Powers, 1907–
Cotton-patch schoolhouse / Susie Powers Tompkins.
p.   cm.
ISBN 0-8173-0563-7
1. Tompkins, Susie Powers, 1907–   . 2. Teachers—Alabama—
Marengo County—Biography. 3. Education, Rural—Alabama—Marengo
County—History. 4. Marengo County (Ala.)—History. I. Title.
LA2317.T66A3   1991
370.19′346′09761392—dc20   91-23331

British Library Cataloguing-in-Publication Data available

Contents

CONTENTS
vi

Acknowledgments

I wish to express special thanks to the following:

Frances Summersell, a very close friend, who edited and advised me on this book;

Bill Tompkins, my late husband, who encouraged me and took me back to see the little schoolhouse so I could photograph it;

Edward E. Morgan, mutual friend, who gave advice and help;

Margaret Searcy, author and teacher, who offered her expert advice;

Lyda Black, instructor at Shelton State Community College, who typed, edited, revised, and offered professional advice;

To my two children, who showed interest, help, and encouragement while this book was being written; and last, but not least, to

Members of The University of Alabama Press, especially to Malcolm MacDonald and Zig Zeigler, for their patience, advice, and interest.

COTTON-PATCH
SCHOOLHOUSE

1

A Familiar Road
Brings Back Memories

ON THAT WARM SEPTEMBER MORNING IN 1926 I DROVE our Model T Ford up and down the hills of a little country road in Marengo County, Alabama, and was completely happy. At the top of each hill, I would cut off the engine and coast to save gasoline.

I should have been scared to death—not of coasting (the little car was going only fifteen miles an hour and there was no traffic)—but because at age eighteen, I was going forth, with no experience, to teach in a small, one-teacher school consisting of five grades and eight children.

I did not think this lack of experience imposed any problem because Miss Bunker, the county supervisor, whom I had met the week before at the teachers' institute, had promised to help me. She was jolly and friendly, and I had liked her immediately. I think the feeling was mutual, but I got the distinct impression that she was a little surprised at my youthful appearance. She had eyed me up and down, then asked,

"Susie, dear, how old are you?"

"Eighteen, ma'am."

"Any courses in education?"

"Well, I don't think—that is—no ma'am, not if they have to do with teaching."

She sighed. "Well, don't worry, dear, we'll work it out." As she confessed to me later, she had immediately decided to spend much more than her allotted time in that little one-teacher school. But Miss Bunker was new in the community, and no one had informed her that in winter there would be times when she could not get her car within several miles of our school. She could have gotten there by horseback, of course, but she tipped the scales at nearly two hundred pounds and riding a horse was about the last thing she ever intended to do. If we could have foreseen the year ahead, we would have known that there would be long periods when the children and I would be completely isolated to learn what we might and get by as best we could.

At that moment, however, there was no room in my curly head for problems. It was too full of happy thoughts about making some money, which would enable me to return to college for my sophomore year. Anyway, what was there to worry about? I had started my education in a one-teacher school, and my teacher, Mrs. Minnie O'Neal had not five but eight grades. Though youthful for a widow, she was mature, experienced, resolute, and intimidating. I well remembered the baseball bat she kept back of her desk, and I hoped I would have no need for such a weapon.

As I thought back over those years, I decided that one way Mrs. O'Neal got through the day with so many grades was that she saw to it no time was wasted. When a class was called up to the recitation bench, the pupils knew that if they didn't know their lessons, severe punishment would be an absolute certainty. While one class recited, the others were busy in preparation.

In Mrs. O'Neal's class, we worked just as hard at our desks and wasted no time with words. We had signals. Holding up one finger meant that the pupil needed help (and it had better be for a good reason), two fingers meant a trip to the outhouse, and three was for a drink of water. (We all drank from the same bucket and used the same dipper.)

Mrs. O'Neal certainly had the parents on her side. They said to one another proudly, "We have a fine teacher. Strict, too. We like that."

What they did not know was that Mrs. O'Neal was sweeter than usual her first year there and was making every effort to control her temper. The reason was that she had set her cap for our community's most eligible bachelor, Mr. Marvin Peacock, and she did not want any gossip to reach him that would be detrimental to her character. She did get him, and there was a summer wedding.

When Mrs. O'Neal (Peacock) returned for her second year of teaching at Old Spring Hill, her disposition had undergone a complete change. One would think marital bliss would affect her manners. They were affected all right, but for the worse. She had a twelve-year-old daughter, Elmer, who was always into mischief. At the least provocation, Mrs. O'Neal, as we continued to call her, would slap Elmer so hard that her handprint showed for hours.

The old homemade desks that we used seated two, and Elmer shared one with Pete Allen. One day they lifted the lid and put their heads under it. Although I don't know what went on, we could hear giggles. Mrs. O'Neal stopped her lesson, tiptoed back to that desk, and mashed the lid down on their heads with all her strength. She finally let up when they screamed with pain. She dusted her hands and marched back to her lesson without ever looking to see what damage she had done. Needless to say, there was a divorce the following summer, and Mr. Marvin Peacock and his relatives moved to another state. The next year, much to our relief, we had a new teacher.

I still remember that as a small child I had been eager to enter first grade; consequently, I was terribly disappointed when I reached the right age and an illness prevented my doing so. I suddenly came down with a high fever, and our family doctor was baffled. What he had diagnosed as a simple case of biliousness proved to be much more serious. My fever went very high and did not respond to the usual treatments of the time, which were quinine and calomel. Other doctors were called in and were equally baffled; I still recall how hot I was. My grandfather continually brought in buckets of cool water from the well, and my grandmother sat by the bed and sponged by body. My father sent to Demopolis, the largest town in Marengo County, for ice. An ice cap was kept on my forehead around the clock. After about ten days, the fever went away as suddenly as it had come and left me lying pale and weak. Now my family began to tempt me with nourishing food to build up my strength.

One day my mother said, "Maybe you'd enjoy coming to the table to eat." I held on to the bedpost and slid to the floor.

"I can't walk," I said.

"You're just weak," they said. "We'll help you."

But I was right. I couldn't walk.

Next day, with my father carrying me, we boarded the train for Selma, the nearest medical center. After much consultation, the doctors said to my parents, "There have been some outbreaks around the country of a new childhood disease called infantile paralysis. We think your little girl may have had it." They prescribed bed rest and nourishing food.

"In time, we think she may walk. Give her a chance, and if she does, bring her back to us as she no doubt will need a brace."

After several months, and much effort, I finally managed to limp a few yards without help. Then followed a series of trips to Selma for brace fitting to keep my ankle straight because paralysis of one of the leaders had made it begin to turn. Now I began to think of school.

"If I don't go to school, I'll never learn to read," I wailed. I was almost seven.

My mother quoted the doctors: "They say you may not go now, but next fall you'll be ready."

My grandmother told my parents not to worry because she would teach me.

"Ma," said my father, partly in jest, "when did you learn how to teach?"

"I'll have you to know, Davy," as she called my father, "that when your Pa went off to the Civil War, if I had not taught your older brothers, they would not have even learned to read. There were no schools and no teachers."

"Can we begin right now, Grandma?" I begged.

"It won't be long—I promise. You know how busy we are now putting up food for winter."

"How about at night, Grandma?"

"Yes, that's when we'll have our lessons. But we'll have to wait for the weather to cool. It is terribly hot at night now, and you know how we must sit on the front gallery [as we called the porch] until the house cools off."

I did know that, and I looked forward to those nightly gatherings when we children lay on pallets and listened to the adults talk over the events of the day and tell stories as they rocked back and forth in their rocking chairs. They had become so adept at telling family stories that ancestors seemed to come to life again and long-gone days were relived. The stories were as good as if not better than those in my storybooks.

We did have our lessons when the weather cooled, and we did them by the light of a fire and kerosene lamp. We had a little black girl, Rosa, given to us by a family that was overburdened with children. My parents felt responsible for Rosa's education, and my grandmother, as long as she was able, taught Rosa until the child had a very good elementary education. Rosa was my first classmate.

As soon as supper was over and the dishes washed, Rosa and I would take our slates and pencils and, with Rosa pulling me in my little wagon which I preferred to the big wheelchair, hurried to my grandparents' room. Grandma first taught us our ABC's and then how to spell the easy, rhyming words. By learning to spell, we learned to read. It was an antiquated method, but it worked, and by Christmas Rosa and I were reading every easy book in the house. No accomplishment in my life had ever delighted me so much. In the fall, I was able to enter school in Old Spring Hill and because of my grandmother's help, I went through two grades during my first year with Mrs. O'Neal.

Just when my family was feeling relieved and happy about me, another disaster struck. It was in the form of a tiny insect called the boll weevil, which bored into cotton bolls so that the cotton never opened. A little before the turn of the century, this weevil crossed the Mexican border and attacked the vast cotton fields of Texas. In time, it moved on to Louisiana, Mississippi, and then Alabama. The whole economy of the South was threatened. When my father had his first cotton-crop failure, his father said to him, "Now Dave, plant other crops—no more cotton. Else you might lose all of your savings."

My grandfather was right, of course, but it was not easy for my father to change. He had invested in all the equipment for growing cotton. Also, living on our farm were some of the best cotton pickers in the county, including one very old black man who broke records by picking four hundred pounds a day. Other pickers would say to him, "No wonder you beats us. You so stooped you already down close to de cotton stalks." Other inducements to my father to "plant one more time" were the circulars that came almost daily in the mail from insecticide companies saying they had come up with a formula to control the boll weevil. In the end, my father went broke and the weevil continued to thrive.

My parents felt they were still young enough to make a second start and earn enough money to achieve their two lifelong goals: to own a home and educate their children. They decided to make a change from independent farmer to employee.

A Mr. Shedd from Chicago had purchased a large tract of land called Egypt, the last large plantation in the area. We knew the place well because the Eppes estate, where we then lived, joined it, and some of the former owners of Egypt were friends of my parents. Even when I was a baby, my father would put me on a pillow in front of his saddle, and with these friends we would ride over the plantation. It then was sixteen hundred acres, but my father had known it when it was even larger. When Mr. Shedd purchased this vast acreage, he told his new business acquaintances that he knew nothing about farming in the South and even less about the black people who were so necessary to the operation of such a plantation.

Egypt, the sixteen-hundred-acre plantation where I grew up

He then asked whether they knew of anyone who was experienced along these lines and might be interested in the job of helping him.

"Mr. Dave Powers would be an excellent choice, if you could get him," they told him. "He has been a successful farmer in this area all of his adult life, and so was his father before him. He has just had a loss from the boll weevil and for that reason might be interested."

Mr. Shedd then made frequent visits to our home during which he and my father sat on the front gallery discussing all aspects of the job. Finally, my parents agreed that the benefits offered were too good to be turned down and the decision was made. We moved to Egypt, and to this day I feel that growing up there afforded me some of the richest and most wonderful experiences of my life.

2

My First Horse

FOR THE FIRST TIME I HAD A HORSE OF MY OWN. Doctors who had cared for me during my polio advised my parents to see that I spent much time in the open air and sun. Knowing how I loved horses, my father would allow me to ride behind him while he made his daily trips around the plantation. As a result, I became brown and strong. One day we watched the wild horses that roamed the big pasture. They had never been touched by a human hand, and when they saw us, they would take off following their leader, an iron-gray stallion.

"Daddy," I said wistfully, "do you think I can ever ride one of those?" He looked at me in shocked surprise.

"Have you lost your mind? Even the man we hired to try to break some of them can hardly stay on!" Then, seeing my face, he added more kindly, "Don't worry. We'll find you something to ride."

The next day a small horse, purchased in Clarke County, was tethered to our front gate. Rosa saw him first and told me.

I was in such a hurry to see the horse that Rosa had to hold my skirt to keep me from falling. A note was pinned to the bridle. We read: "This is Clark. He is to Susie from the 'Plantation.'" That last word stumped us. Then we took it by syllables as Grandma had taught us.

"Plan-ta-tion." "Plantation!" I exclaimed. "Rosa, the plantation has given me a horse! Isn't that wonderful!"

Rosa stepped back so she could get a good look at the poor animal. His head was down and his eyes were closed; his mane and tail were a mass of cockleburs; his ribs showed and his hip bones stuck out and he had a set-fast in his back. Rosa shook her head.

In the meantime, I had pulled the horse's head up and kissed him on the nose. "Lawd, Miss Susie, don' kiss a hoss!" But I did not hear Rosa. The horse had opened his eyes, and we were looking at each other. Right then a relationship between us was born that was rare for horse and rider.

Clark was very gentle, and for the first time my parents allowed me to ride around the quarter pasture alone. But my father knew horses. "Clark may not be so gentle when he gets his health back so we must watch him," he cautioned. Maybe Clark was an exception to the rule because of all the attention we gave him. He got as round and as beautiful as a circus pony, yet he remained gentle, at least with children. He hated men, and whenever one got on him, he would buck. My father thought it was because someone had mistreated him. As many as four children could climb on his back at once. We could slide off his tail and climb under him. Still, he was gentle and remained that way with my friends and me as long as he lived. Yes, Clark was a very unusual horse and I loved him with all my heart.

Roads were bad in that area in winter, and transportation

Clark, my first horse, so poor his ribs showed

was a problem for us. My parents solved this by having one of the old black men, whom they fully trusted, usually either Uncle Reuben or Uncle Cajer, take me to school in the buggy as long as that was possible. When the mud became too deep for the buggy, one of them would accompany me on horseback, and I would ride Clark. When winter weather prevented that, I would board in the village with Mrs. Eppes, a leader in the community and an accomplished artist. She gave me my first lessons in painting, which many years later provided me with both pleasure and income.

As a whole, I remember those as very happy years, and one summer when I was about ten years old an event occurred that was to change my life. Young Dr. Abernathy, the village physician, came to our house with an exciting piece of news. A Dr. Marcus Skinner, who had won much recognition for his surgery on victims of polio, was moving his practice to Selma. Dr. Abernathy wanted my parents' permission to take me to see this doctor. Of course, they were grateful. An appointment was made, and we went by train to Selma. After an examination, Dr. Skinner said he could help me, and an operation was

How I fed him! Soon he became round and pretty.

arranged. It was so successful that even though I would always have a limp, I never had to wear a brace again. I especially remember the first pair of black patent leather slippers I could wear instead of the heavy, high-top shoes. All my life I was to remember those slippers as the most precious wearing apparel I ever owned.

I was able to complete five grades in four years at the one-teacher school in Old Spring Hill, but then we were faced with another dilemma. Because of lack of money and pupils, there would be no sixth grade so it was arranged that I would go by train to Laurel, Mississippi, to live with my maternal grandmother during school months. The year was 1918, and soldiers coming home from World War I brought into the country a deadly virus known as Spanish influenza. Doctors had no knowledge then of ways to control it, and there was a great epidemic. Sometimes whole families would succumb to the disease. No sooner had I gotten settled in school than it had to close. People shivered behind shut doors, and I was not allowed to play with neighborhood children. I think if I were ever to be homesick it should have been during those lonely days when I sat in my grandmother's upstairs dormer window and watched the continuous funeral processions pass by on the way to the nearby cemetery.

Later that year, the influenza struck our family, and my Uncle Adolphus, who was visiting, took the virus and died. Another uncle from Alabama, Uncle Hugh, came to the funeral, and because there was no prospect of schools reopening, I accompanied him home on the train.

As long as I live, I shall never forget that trip. Like all travelers during the epidemic, we were compelled to wear face masks. In Meridian, Mississippi, where we had a long layover between trains, guards were posted all around and they would not allow us to remove the masks, even for a bite to eat or a drink of water. That was very hard on a child, and I thought I might die, but we made it home. For me there was no school that year.

3

My First Love Affair

AS MY LITTLE FORD RATTLED ALONG THE COUNTRY road, many memories raced through my mind. Of all the people who worried about my missing a year of school, it seemed that Mammy Lou, our old black midwife on Egypt, worried most. She expressed it this way:

"Po' lil' Miss wid de twisted leg. She needs to git dat eddication case dey ain' no man gwine take keer o' her. She won' neber mahhy." When my father heard her say this, he glared at her, something he had never done before.

"What has her leg got to do with marriage?"

"Ought not te have nuttin to do wid hit, Boss, but mens is funny dataway. You'll see."

"Yes, and you'll see," said my father. He thought I was beautiful and perfect and would be a prize for any man. When I did marry, Mammy Lou was not alive to attend, and I was sorry.

Another person who worried about my missing school was Uncle Hugh's new wife, whom I called Aunt Bessie. She would invite me for long visits, and from her library she selected a very good reading program of such old classics as Charles Dickens's *David Copperfield*, Mark Twain's *Tom Sawyer*, and *Huckleberry Finn*, Louisa May Alcott's *Little Women*, and many more. When my visit was over, she would select books for me to take home, and my father, also an avid reader, would have me read to him at night.

The next year I went back to Laurel, Mississippi, where I completed junior high school. Then I went to Moundville, Alabama, where I lived with my Aunt Frances, to complete the Hale County high school there. Those were good years, and two events of that time stand out in my mind.

One was the excavation by the University of Alabama of the Indian mounds located in and around Moundville, many along the banks of the Black Warrior River. There are some forty of these mounds, the largest of which is about sixty feet high. The excavation brought up many beautiful and often amazing artifacts made by this tribe of Indians, known as the Mound Builders. Today the area is a state park with a museum that houses the objects, which reveal much about the culture of a people whose life-style had been buried for many centuries beneath the ground.

The other event that I remember was important only to me and the young man who was the object of my affections. For the first time, I fell desperately in love. All my life I had had little boys for playmates and sometimes claimed them for sweethearts, but nothing had been like this.

It was my first day in the school, and at the desk across from me sat a young man whom I thought was utterly handsome. It was love at first sight for both of us, and we paid attention to little else that went on in the classroom that day. When school was out, he came to my desk, timidly took my hand, and introduced himself.

"I'm David Hopper," he said. "You're new here, aren't you?"

"Yes, David, I am. I'm Susie." I gathered up my books to go.

"Where do you live?" he asked, taking the books from me.

"Why, I don't know the name of the street. Maybe you know my family here, Mr. and Mrs. Pat Davis. She's my aunt."

"Know them! Miss Frances used to teach me!"

Just then someone called, "Wait for me."

It was Kitty, one of my new friends.

"Kitty! Do you know each other?"

"Sure," said David, stepping between us and taking her books too. Kitty lived just down the street from my aunt, and we had walked to school together.

"Where do you live, David?" I asked.

"Just two streets from your aunt by the railroad."

After that the three of us walked home together almost every day and ended up in front of our gate. If Aunt Frances were not busy, she would invite us in for ice cream or some other treat. If we walked home with Kitty, her mother would serve us something. We were always hungry after school. Those were long, lazy days, and I felt as if I were living in a dream. When Christmas came, I almost hated to go home for the holidays.

"I'll bet you've got a boyfriend there waiting," teased David.

"There is a boy I grew up with, James, but he's working in Florida. Anyway, we're just friends," I responded.

Sometimes Aunt Frances made me sit down for a serious talk. One evening the subject was dating.

"I'm afraid you and David are seeing each other too much," she said. "It shows in your schoolwork. Don't you think you should date just on weekends and save the week nights for your studies?"

I hung my head. I knew she was right. "I'll tell David," I said, "and we'll do that."

David and I did not usually have many problems in our relationship, but in the spring, we had one that had serious consequences. A boy I had dated and liked asked if I would accompany him to a school party. I could not honestly tell him I had a date because David had not asked me although I felt sure he would. Finally, I told the boy I would let him know.

I sat by the window and watched for David. Why didn't he come or send a note and ask me for that date? Aunt Frances knew I was worried so she finally asked what the trouble was, and I told her.

"Susie," she said, "I think at sixteen you should not settle down to one boy."

I appreciated her advice and interest. She had been a wonderful teacher of young people, and I knew she understood a sixteen-year-old's first love, but I just did not want to date anyone else.

I could not understand why David had not asked me for a date because he knew how much I wanted to go to that party. What I did not know was that he had gone out of town with his father on a job. His father worked on the railroad.

Finally, the friend who asked for the date came by and I had to give him an answer. I said I would go and immediately regretted it. I was perfectly miserable and had no fun at the party. David was not there, and when I got a chance, I asked David's brother why he had not come to the party.

"David and Daddy missed the last train home. He let Mom know by code—said for me to ask you to the party, but when I went by, Miss Frances said you had a date."

"I didn't know what else to do."

The next day David was not at school, and when I asked his brother the reason, he shrugged his shoulders and said, "Says he's not coming back anymore—going to join the navy."

I could hardly wait for the noon hour to come. I took off for home in a hurry with Kitty running behind and calling, "Wait! What's the rush?" When we reached home, I went in the back room and fell across the bed. I did not just cry, I sobbed.

Aunt Frances, who had followed with Kitty, asked her, "What in the world is the matter?" They asked me, and I told them. "David's not coming back; he's going to join the navy."

Aunt Frances sat on the side of the bed. She looked very serious. "Listen, Susie, I know David's father; I can't believe he'll allow David to join any branch of the service until he finishes high school. That would be foolish."

I sat up and wiped my eyes. "Maybe his father won't know it until it's done."

Aunt Frances could be much fun. Her eyes began to twinkle, and she explained: "Now, Susie, dry your eyes and listen. A lady came by this morning selling poetry she had written when she was disappointed in love. I'll bet that now you could make money like that."

I began to laugh. "How would I do that?"

"Why, write something like this—" and my aunt made up a funny little rhyme.

Kitty and I laughed so hard there was no room for tears. Already life began to look sunny again.

"Kitty," said my aunt, "call your mother and tell her you are going to eat with us; I have plenty." Then she whispered to Kitty as she showed her where the phone was.

"You mustn't leave us now, I'll fix you a plate."

I went to the washstand and washed my eyes. I began to feel

better, and when I sat down to Aunt Frances's good hot corn bread, turnip greens, and pot roast, my appetite returned.

On the way back to school, we caught up with David's brother.

"Well, the navy idea didn't work out for David," he told us. "Dad said if he stopped school, there was a job for him on the railroad but no navy, not yet anyway."

When we were in sight of the school, the bell rang. David was on the porch waiting for me. When he spoke, I knew things were not the same between us.

"When school is out, we need to talk," was all he said.

When the dismissal bell rang, I whispered to Kitty, "You go on home without me." I met David at the back door, and we walked down the hill together, found an isolated spot, and sat on the grass. For a while we did not speak, but he reached over and kissed me on the cheek. It was not a kiss of anger; it was more a kiss of good-bye, and we both felt sad.

"Why did you do it?" he finally asked.

"I didn't want to. I put it off thinking I would hear from you, but I never did."

"As you know now, we missed the last train home that night and I had no way of calling you."

"David, you and I never discussed plans for the future. What do you want to do with your life?"

"Why, I don't know. Get a good job, I guess, and make some money. Someday I'd marry and have children. Isn't that the thing to do?"

"Why, yes, it is. I want those things, too, but first I'd like a college education. Don't you want one?"

"Why, yes, but I'm not smart in books like you. I hear you'll be the class valedictorian."

"David! It's what you want and are willing to work for. There are many wonderful things out there in the world to learn about."

"I guess so." He stood up. "If you ever need anything that I can do, will you let me know?"

"Yes, David, and remember one thing. You'll always be dear to me."

He walked on down the hill. I brushed back the tears, but I knew it was best that we part.

In time I dated other people and so did he. I felt a kind of freedom that I had missed. The next year David fell in love and married. They had a big family; he never graduated from high school.

4

I Go to College

KITTY AND I GRADUATED FROM HALE COUNTY HIGH, and that fall we entered Alabama College, a charming little girls' school in Montevallo, located in the heart of Alabama and surrounded by the foothills of the Appalachians. The school, its beauty, and its wonderful faculty and student body were everything I had dreamed about, and I had never been so happy in school. Now I was learning the true meaning of an education.

In the spring the greatest jolt in my educational career came in a letter from my parents. Mr. Shedd had gone into bankruptcy, and my family was leaving Egypt, moving to Old Spring Hill. Their financial difficulties meant that it would be impossible for them to send me back to college in the fall.

I did not know which hurt more, giving up Egypt or giving up college. No matter what hardships I had to endure in the winters, there had always been Egypt, with its rolling meadows and horses to ride, to look forward to in summers.

I decided there was nothing I could do about leaving Egypt,

but I refused to accept giving up college. I could earn money—
I knew I could. When I got home, I tried to find a job, and
friends tried for me, but to no avail. Toward the end of summer, it seemed I must accept the fact that in the rural section
of Alabama where we lived there was no way for a girl so
young to find gainful employment, and I became thoroughly
miserable.

To add to these sorrows, Clark had gotten out of the small
pasture we used and gone to Egypt. But he went the back way,
where the gate was closed. His hoofprints showed that he had
waited there for some time, no doubt expecting someone to
let him in. Finally, thirsty, he went to a nearby pool for a
drink, but it was drying up and very boggy. Clark went the way
of many animals that get in a bog, and he died there. My
family said I could feel assured that he did not suffer much.
Uncle Reuben, with a team of mules, pulled him out and
buried him. I had so many problems now that I tried not to
think of Clark.

One hot August afternoon, I was sitting on our porch when
a car pulled up to the gate and Mr. Dick Allen, a longtime
family friend, got out and came up the walk. We shook hands,
and I invited him to sit down. I explained that my parents
were not at home.

"It's you I came to see," he said, pulling a rocker near the
swing where I was sitting. "I know how hard you've been trying to find a job, and I have something in mind." Then he
added with a laugh, "But I'm not sure I'm being a real friend to
tell you about it."

"Oh, Mr. Dick, if it's a job, please tell me. I don't care how
hard it is."

"Well," he said, "I know how much you want to continue
college, and you can think this over. Down in the piney

woods, there is a little school in need of a teacher. The building is just one room and very crude—"

"I'll take it," I interrupted.

"Now wait," he said with a laugh. "There are eight children
and five grades—too many, even for an experienced teacher.
As chairman of the board, I can get the job for you but—"

"Oh, Mr. Dick, I can learn! I've got to have that job."

"It's on one of the worst roads in the country," he said,
ignoring my remarks. "That alone has defeated most teachers
who have tried it."

"But Mr. Dick, roads wouldn't defeat me because I can ride
a horse. I'll take the job."

"Yes, but there are other drawbacks. It's just a seven-month
school and pays only seventy dollars a month. Would that be
enough to get you back to college?"

"If I saved every cent, it would have to."

"Well," he sighed, "there is one bright side. We do have a
wonderful supervisor who would work with you, but it wouldn't
be easy."

"That's all right," I said, taking the contract out of his hand
for fear he would change his mind. He reluctantly handed me
his pen, and with a sigh of relief I signed on the dotted line.

Mr. Dick stood up and put on his hat.

"Now Susie, you must promise me one thing, and I mean
this—that you and your father will ride down there and at
least look the building over."

"Yes, sir, we surely will, if you insist. But Mr. Dick, I can
tell you one thing. I'm going to make you proud of me. I'm
going to teach in that little school, and I'm going back to
college." And that was how I came to be driving down the
little country road on that September morning.

My father and I had complied with Mr. Dick's wishes and

had driven the sixteen miles to inspect the school building. We found it to be every bit as crude as Mr. Dick had said— one long room with no ceiling, homemade desks and benches, and a potbellied stove near the center. It was situated out in a cotton field with no other buildings in sight. These things bothered me not at all, but what did bother me very much was that there was no outhouse!

"Daddy," I exclaimed after he and I had searched in vain for one, "what in the world do they do?"

"I have no idea," he said, "but we're going to find out." For that purpose, we stopped at a farmhouse belonging to a Mr. Douglas, who was one of the school's patrons. When my father brought up the matter of the outhouse and asked what one did when the need arose, Mr. Douglas looked rather embarrassed, scratched his head, and said, "Well, I reckon they go the nearby woods an' set over a log."

I was horrified because in the woods there were snakes, and snakes were my one fear. My father asked if an outhouse could be built. The man pondered the question and frowned with concern.

"Sir, I might as well tell you the truth. The school jes ain't got no money. With what we had, we fixed the roof. We had to dig a little into our own pockets to repair the well casing. We aimed to build a outhouse, but looks like first we got to raise the money, somehow, for the lumber."

Then my father came up with a solution. He had a good shed which he did not use. If he tore it down and hauled the lumber to the school, could the patrons do the building? Mr. Douglas said we could depend on it, and he personally would see that it was ready for the opening of school.

Again I was happy, and I sang merrily as I drove toward my school that morning. I was even relaxed enough to enjoy the beautiful scenery through which I was passing. It was part of a strip of land running through the state known as Alabama's Black Belt, where the soil was so dark and rich that in summer cattle grazed on the greenest of pastures, where crops were lush with no need for fertilizer, and where the finest hay in the country was made.

The plantation Egypt lay in this part of the Black Belt, and the road over which I was traveling ran through much of it. Every tree, every fence post of the plantation was familiar to me because during my childhood and youth I had ridden with my father over every acre of this lovely land. I had not been back to Egypt since we moved because I knew nothing would be the same as when we lived there, and from what I could now see from the road, I knew I was right.

The cabins in view were empty except for those occupied by four old people who refused to move. They had been born there as slaves and they had never known any other home so they were allowed to stay.

The doors of the cabins had been left open to bang in the wind and the clotheslines were bare. Many beautiful old washpots sat idle by the wells, and I was sure that some had water, stale and turning green, in which mosquitoes were hatching. I could not see any of the usual crops growing, and the hay fields were full of wildflowers and jimsonweed. As much as I hated seeing what was happening on Egypt, when I reached the big gate I could hardly refrain from turning in.

"This is no time to think back or to be homesick," I said half aloud, but I promised myself that some Saturday I would spend a whole day on Egypt to say good-bye to that place which I loved more than any other spot on earth. In spite of all the changes, Egypt would always hold a certain fascination for me as I thought of its rolling green meadows and clumps of pretty trees and its rich valley with a creek winding through it, bordered by cottonwood trees whose leaves were in perpetual motion, even when there was no breeze.

As these memories raced through my mind, it struck me that there was a certain irony in the beauty of the Black Belt because the very dark, rich soil that created it, that soil so prized by farmers, was the reason for the bad winter roads that would in time prevent my driving from home as I was now doing. The texture of the soil was fine and loamy, and continuous winter rains made it into such a sticky mess that it would cling to wheels of carts, buggies, and wagons. Drivers occasionally had to get out and clean it from between the spokes with a pickax or they would bog down.

In better-cared-for sections, where roads had been graveled (a fairly new procedure in Marengo County), people could manage fairly well in winter. According to Mr. Dick, the patrons of my school had long begged for such a road so that their children could ride buses to consolidated educational centers as other children were doing in some sections, but the people were told that until the county had more money they would have to make do with the little school building they had and one teacher. I was that teacher, and even now I was making my way to their community, totally unaware of the many surprises that lay in store for me.

5

I Meet the Children
and Reverend Milford

A S I WENT OVER THE LAST HILL AND THE SCHOOL CAME in view, I gave an audible, "Oh!" and put on the brakes. Then my eyes fell on a point beyond the building. There it stood, the outhouse, the only thing to break the horizon in the sea of white cotton—tall, slender, and a bit crooked, probably a one-holer, but it was there and that was what mattered. On the tiny front porch of the school building the children stood gazing in my direction.

"Holy mackerel!" I gasped, again slowing up. "Why, some of those children are taller than I am!" There were only eight, but they looked like a multitude.

They were not at all what I had expected. Perhaps they would think me too young to teach and be difficult to handle. The prospects worried me for a moment, then I decided that should this be the case I would shift the burden to the broad shoulders of Miss Bunker and seek her advice. In the mean-time I would be as prim and dignified as possible. I was very sorry that my hair was not done up in a bun on top of my

I go forth on my first job of teaching

head. I had tried to accomplish this for about an hour the night before, but my hair was long, thick, and curly. In the end I had given up and tied it back with a ribbon in my usual fashion.

I drove slowly, considering my predicament. When I reached the school, I turned into the yard. Almost before I could stop, the children were off the porch and surrounding the car. They all smiled shyly. They certainly did not look like difficult children. A tall boy, whom I took to be the oldest, opened the car door for me while the girls gathered up the books and my purse; the youngest, the only other boy, clasped my hand. These acts of friendliness were what I desperately needed at that moment.

"How nice of you to come out to meet me," I said, and smiled at them. Then the oldest girl, Debra, who seemed to be the most mature of the group and was a sister of the oldest boy, spoke: "We have been here waiting for you since daylight."

"You have!" I exclaimed, looking at my watch. It was not yet eight o'clock, and school did not open until eight-thirty.

"Then you must be tired." They did not comment but followed me into the schoolhouse and stacked the books neatly on the teacher's desk, which stood at the far end of the room. Only then did the little boy whom I came to know as Toby let go of my hand. He wanted to inspect the books.

"You will learn to read in these," I said, pointing to some preprimers. "That is, if you haven't already learned to read. Have you?"

"No, ma'am," he said, turning the pages of a preprimer, "but I know my ABC's." Then he added, "There are only forty-one pages in this book." I made a mental note that Toby could count, too. The other children crowded around the desk, anxious to see which books they would study.

"I'll tell you what," I suggested. "Let's sit down together and get acquainted. When I know what grades you are in, I can better show you your books."

I pulled my chair, homemade but sturdy, from behind my desk and with the children's help arranged benches in a semicircle. Only one girl, who was sixteen and named Minnie, did not join us. She stayed by the window, her eyes riveted on the road. Debra whispered to me, "Minnie's got a beau named Cluster. He drives a logging truck and will be along directly."

The other children giggled, and Cammie, the Milford girl who was in fifth grade, laughed out loud. She was a plump little girl with merry gray eyes, and I came to know her as my clown.

I took a good look at Minnie. She was a beautiful girl with a head full of dark curls and a figure well matured for her years. I decided it would be wise not to bother Minnie for the moment.

There was a rolling blackboard nearby and on it an eraser and chalk, probably left by the previous teacher. I pulled the board over to us and wrote, "Miss Susie Powers." Then I pronounced it and said, "You may call me Miss Powers or Miss Susie." I reached for my register and a pen. "Now I'm anxious to know your names." I wrote their names, ages, grades, and addresses as they gave them. There were four from one family, the Milfords, two from the Douglas family, and two from the Tuckers. Toby Douglas, as I knew, was in first grade; Lily, the youngest Milford, in third; Ellie Douglas and Cammie Milford in fifth; Dimmie Milford in seventh; and Dan and Debra Tucker and Minnie Milford in eighth.

"So much for business," I said, putting the register aside. "Now I'd like you to tell me what you enjoy at school."

Minnie, still by the window, spoke softly: "I don't enjoy nuthin'." It was not spoken impudently but with complete sincerity. "You don't?" I asked, trying not to sound surprised. "I can understand that because there was a subject in school that I did not like."

"What didn't you like?" asked Minnie, joining the group for the first time but still keeping an eye on the road. "When you girls are in high school, you will take a subject called home economics. That is learning to cook, sew, and keep house. I never did well with that. My cakes always fell, and the clothes I made never fit. I did not like it very much."

Debra spoke up. "I think I would like that. My Ma lets me bake cakes sometimes. I like chauk'let the best. Sometime I'll bring you a piece."

For the first time I took a good look at Debra. She was a

very attractive brunette with a perpetual smile and brown eyes that sparkled when she talked. I could already see that she had leadership qualities.

"Oh, please do bring me a piece of your cake because chocolate's my favorite cake, too."

For the first time Dan spoke. I could see why he hesitated to talk because he stammered and stuttered, but finally he managed to ask, "W-W-What do the boys take?"

"They take what they call shop. You know, learning to build things."

"Dan builds real good now," said Debra. "He helped Pa build a cow shed. He helps Pa with a lot of things. That's why he can't go to school much."

Dan seemed pleased with the compliment. Perhaps he also felt relieved that his sister had explained why he was still in eighth grade. Dan was a tall, thin boy with a shock of unruly sandy hair. His eyes were pale blue and a bit timid, but they gave one a feeling that he was very sincere. Often his mouth hung open and he looked retarded, but I found that to be far from the truth. He had good ideas, and in time I came to depend on him in many ways.

I was about to continue our conversation when a rumbling sound from the road claimed our attention. Minnie ran back to the window, and all eyes turned in that direction. A logging truck came around the curve in a cloud of dust. It was driven by a young man who waved wildly when he saw Minnie in the window. She waved back until he passed from view. Minnie then turned to rejoin the group, but she stopped short, her hand over her heart.

"It's Pa," she gasped. "He's comin'. If he saw me wave, I-I don't know what he'll do."

Minnie's three younger sisters ran to her and clasped her

around the waist. They all looked as frightened as she. It was plain whose side they were on.

I looked out, too. Yes, no doubt her father had seen her wave because he was making his way to the school, walking with a purpose.

"It would be better if you would all come and sit down," I said, trying to speak with a calmness I did not feel. They came, but they all seemed disturbed. Lily could not keep back the tears. I saw a little stool nearby. I pulled it to my side and told Lily to sit there, then I put my arm around the sobbing child.

I sensed that Lily was a very insecure child, small for her age and very pretty, almost a replica of her oldest sister, Minnie, except that Lily wore her hair long. I wondered who had curled it so beautifully this morning. I learned later that because their mother was so busy with the younger children and other chores, Lily's three older sisters took complete charge of her.

All of the girls, even Minnie, wore homemade gingham dresses, starched, ironed, clean, and plain, but attractive. The two boys were dressed in homemade shirts and long pants. They all gave me the impression that the opening of school was a very important occasion for them.

Lily began to tremble as her father drew nearer. I thought I should try to reassure her.

"Don't be afraid," I said. I wanted to put on a brave front, but if I were not afraid, why did I feel as I thought a general might who was about to lead his troops into battle? I squared my shoulders and prepared for the worst.

A tall man with stooped shoulders came up the steps. He had a Bible under his arm and a walking cane in his hand. I remembered then that the father of the Milford children was a preacher. The door was open because of the hot weather, and he stood there glaring at us. His heavy brows and long mustache that curled at the ends only made him look more like a villain in a wild west movie. He swept off his broad black hat.

"How do you do," I said. "You must be the Reverend Milford."

"I am, and I aimed to come peaceable, bringing the prayer and Scripture reading that any good school ought to open with. Then what do I see? Minnie there, waving at the scoundrel I've forbidden her to speak to. Miss, is this the way you aim to run this school?"

"Reverend Milford," I said, beginning to feel a little anger myself as I looked at the cane, "of course I do not know anything about the relationship of your daughter and the young man. But I can assure you that she did not break any school rules by waving. You see, school is not in session right now. All I was supposed to do today was meet the children and give them a list of textbooks to buy. I was only staying to get acquainted. Won't you sit down with us?"

He flopped down, opened his Bible, and read aloud. Then he got down and prayed about the wrath of the Lord against sinners. The prayer went on and on, and the longer he prayed the louder he got. Sweat ran down his face and dripped on the floor. The children got restless, especially little Toby sitting next to him. I saw Toby's bare foot slide across the floor to the puddle. Then he dipped his big toe in and drew pictures. I raised my head enough to see whether Reverend Milford had observed what Toby was doing. His eyes were shut tight so I bowed my head again and breathed a sigh of relief. After what seemed an aeon, the prayer came to an end.

Reverend Milford then went to my desk and looked at the books. "I don't see no Bible!"

"It will be here tomorrow. As I said, today is not a regular day. I plan to open each day with a reading of the Scriptures. Some are so beautiful that I thought the children might memorize them."

"That's better," said the Reverend. Then he began to examine the prices on the textbooks.

"You aim for me to buy these expensive books for four younguns?"

"They will need some if they are to do homework. But I realize that for four children, that would amount to a great deal. Perhaps we can get help for such things." He drew himself up proudly.

"We don't accept no charity." He started for the door, then turned and pointed an accusing finger at me. "Ma'am, if you can't teach 'em what they need to know, you don't b'long here." He then stalked out of the school and down the road. As I watched him go, I had the impression that his shoulders were more stooped than before. Although my sympathies were with Minnie, somewhere deep inside of me a spark of sympathy for this proud, angry man was born. Surely he loved his daughter very much to have shown his emotions so openly.

Then I turned my attention back to the children. They were still very restless, and it seemed impossible to recapture the friendly, eager attention I had had from them earlier. Therefore, I went to my desk to show them the books they had seemed so anxious to examine. They looked at them with lukewarm enthusiasm. After Reverend Milford's outburst about the expense, I thought it wise to feel the others out.

"Do you think your parents will be able to buy these books for you?" The Milfords hung their heads and were silent. Ellie Douglas, a pretty little blonde who had been silent up to now, spoke up: "My Pa asked me to find out what books me and

Toby needed. He goes to town regular to buy cow feed and could get 'em. He said to ask if you needed anything."

"Thank your father for me. I'm sure that sometime we'll need something." This was the first friendly gesture I had had from the patrons. Now I turned to Dan and Debra, who were thumbing through the eighth grade books. As usual, Debra was the spokesperson.

"I-I don't know, Miss Susie, if Pa can buy these books or not, but we'll take the list."

"Well," I said, "maybe we'd better call it a day." Lily reached over and took my hand.

"Can't we stay a little longer?"

"Well, there is something we might talk about if you will all come back and sit down." This time Minnie came too.

"This room," I said, "needs something. The walls seem so bare."

Dimmie, the Milford just younger than Minnie, held up her hand.

"Dimmie," I said, "holding up your hand when you wish to speak is a nice thing to do. Then we don't all talk at once. Now, what is it you'd like to say?"

"I think some pictures would look purty on the walls. Minnie kin draw real good."

Minnie hung her head modestly. "Why, Minnie, how nice that would be. Do you have crayons or paints?" I asked.

"I did have some, but my little brother lost 'em."

"Well, I think I have some and some paper too. Dimmie, I'm so glad you thought of it." Dimmie's face lit up at this compliment. She was a thin, sallow-looking little girl, but when she smiled, she was almost pretty. In time, she proved to be the most alert of the Milford girls.

Dan held up his hand. "Yes, Dan?"

"My Ma raises real purty flowers."

"Oh, how nice a vase of flowers would look on my desk! I'll bring a vase. I'd better make a list." I wrote down "vase, crayons, paints, paper, Bible." I surely did not want to forget the Bible and have Reverend Milford after me again. Then I thought of another thing, and I wrote down "globe."

"Boys and girls, have you ever used a globe?" Most whispered, "No ma'am," and shook their heads. "Well, I have one I once used at school. It's round and on a stand. It represents the world and has things painted and drawn on it like countries, oceans, rivers, and cities. The globe is a map of the world. Now I really must go."

Minnie ran over and took my hand.

"I wish I could go home with you."

I said to the others: "Boys and girls, Minnie and I need to go out back and have a talk. Will you do something for me? Put the benches back in order and close the windows and doors. Then if you'll take the books and other things to the car, I'll meet you there. Look, Dan, when Minnie and I go out, lock this back door, please. I have two sets of keys. Will you be the keeper of one set? If you get here any morning before I do, you can open up for us."

I handed him two keys on a ring. He seemed pleased with the responsibility. "Want me to lock the front door, too?"

"Yes, please, when you all have finished. And, oh, I almost forgot to tell you. We stay all day tomorrow so unless you live close enough to walk home to lunch—we have an hour— better bring a bite to eat."

Minnie and I went out, and the others began doing as I had asked.

"Minnie," I said when we were alone, "I do have some understanding of how you feel. I am the oldest girl in my family

The only other building was the outhouse. It sat behind the school in plain view!

just as you are, and my father was very strict with me. I think fathers hate especially to see their daughters grow up and fall in love for fear of losing them. Your father wants what he thinks is best for you."

"Does your father beat you?" she asked.

"No, but he is very strict about my being in early at night."

"Well, my Pa don't zactly beat me, but he ain't got no call to hate Cluster. He's a good boy."

"I'm sure he is, if you like him so much. But you know I am just here to teach and can't interfere with things like that. I do want to be your friend."

"Thank you, ma'am."

"And I do have one suggestion: Try not to do things to

make your father so angry. Then I think you will be happier. Will you try?"

"Yes'm."

I felt I was on dangerous ground in this discussion with Minnie so I was glad to change the subject.

"Now let's look at our new outhouse." As I thought, it was a one-holer, but it was nice and clean with a barrel of lime and a shovel for sanitary purposes. Over a string hung a mail-order catalog, the usual substitute for tissue in country toilets.

"You children must thank your fathers for building this for us."

"My Pa done a little," said Minnie. "But Mr. Douglas, he done the most."

When we got to the car, I told the other children to thank their fathers. I also thanked them for helping me.

"I think we are going to have a good time together," I said, and for the first time I really believed it.

"We think so, too," said Debra. They all smiled and waved as I drove away from my first day as a teacher.

6

A Glimpse of Home

THE CHILDREN WERE WAVING AS LONG AS I COULD see them in the rear mirror. I turned a curve, hiding them from view, and then my thoughts were my own. I had dreaded this day and thought I would be relieved to have it behind me. Why, then, did I feel a twinge of sadness at parting from those children? The episode with Reverend Milford had given the children and me a togetherness that I had not expected so soon. That had certainly been a strange turn of events.

I did not go straight home as planned but drove a good many miles out of the way to go by the County Board of Education in Linden and, as I had hoped, Miss Bunker was still there. She was in a meeting so I sat outside her door and waited. The opening of school was one of Miss Bunker's busiest days of the year, but when she came out and saw me, she smiled and sat down beside me.

"Well, how did things go?"

"I think things went very well, but we do have a problem." I decided not to tell her yet about Reverend Milford.

"Not with the children, I hope."

"Oh, no. They are sweet children with nice manners. We do have a sixteen-year-old girl who is very much in love and is not at all interested in school, but I don't think she will be a discipline problem. The trouble is that only one family can afford the textbooks."

Miss Bunker wrinkled her brow. "Susie, I have an idea. I know where there is a big secondhand bookstore. When I have finished with these meetings, suppose I go by and see what they have in the way of textbooks. Then, if at all possible, I'll come by your school tomorrow." She rose to go, but I put my hand on her arm.

"Miss Bunker, I'd like your advice about something else."

"Certainly."

"With the older children, I have at least the textbooks to guide me, but we have a little boy in first grade, and I have no idea how to start a child off in reading."

"Then why don't I give you a demonstration at school tomorrow. Do you have any indication that he will be a fast learner?"

"I think perhaps he will. He told me how many pages were in a preprimer, and he knows his ABC's. He seems very intelligent."

"That's good. Then good-bye until tomorrow." In a flash she was gone. It was surprising that one so large could move so fast.

I had not told Miss Bunker that my oldest pupil, Dan, was older than I. I did not think I would tell anyone. If it got back to Dan, it might embarrass him and have an effect on the others. I felt that I had a good teacher-pupil relationship and I wanted to keep it that way.

When I reached home, the good smells from the kitchen

were overwhelming. I hurried out to find my mother and Rosa putting lunch on the table. My father had come home from the store that he was running just to hear about my first day.

We were a family of three girls. I was the oldest. A few years younger was Elizabeth, whom we called "Bur." Just today she had started going by bus to the Linden high school and had not yet arrived home. Grace Marie, nicknamed "Wee," was the baby, born to my parents late in life. She was running around, begging me to play with her. It was difficult to make her understand that I had no time for playing today so I picked her up and put her in her high chair. Then from the platter of golden brown fried chicken, I found a drumstick for her. She accepted it but still clamored for my attention so I whispered to Rosa: "Could you help us with her? I need to talk with Mamma and Daddy."

"Come on, Wee," urged Rosa. "Let's go find your kitty cat."

Rosa could appease the baby better than anyone. Now Mamma, Daddy, and I settled down to eat and talk. They were very happy about the nice relationship I had established with the children, but when I described the episode with Reverend Milford, both were concerned.

"That is strictly a family problem," cautioned my father, "and it would be very unwise for you to get involved." My mother agreed.

"I'm sure things will come out all right," she said. "Eat your dessert and don't worry."

She had made blackberry cobbler especially for me, knowing it was my favorite. As always, it helped my feelings.

I decided that before preparing for tomorrow's lessons, I would see what I could find in the attic. The globe was there, still intact but very dusty. I found a couple of old vases for Dan's flowers and a large framed map of Alabama and an American flag. I found some watercolors and a brush for Minnie. They were dried up, but I thought they could be soaked. Beside them was a large tablet of watercolor paper, yellowed with age. Now I needed a good book to read to the children on rainy days. I remembered that my mother said our childhood books were stored in a trunk. The trunk was handy but so rusty that the lid had to be pried off. There on top was Louisa May Alcott's *Little Women*, my favorite, but that was a little long to begin with. There was *Pollyanna*, which might do, and under it was *Little Lord Fauntleroy*. I remember one of my teachers reading this book to us and how much we had loved it. I took all three and also some easy stories in case the children became interested in doing some reading on their own.

I was about to close the trunk when something familiar caught my eye—an old tennis racket. I pulled it out and beside it was a ball and my old tennis shoes. The boys might enjoy the ball, and I could use the shoes. I planned to teach the children games, and I could run and play with the high-top tennis shoes to support my ankle. Play! Did those children know how to play? Mostly such children spent their time working on the farm. Well, if they didn't, I would teach them because I still liked to play.

I put all the things that were usable on a table by the front door. On top I put the Bible, which I certainly did not want to forget. Then I went to my room and spread the textbooks out on my desk. It seemed wise to start with the hardest—eighth grade. I picked up the history book and read.

History of Alabama—how wonderful—it was a subject I had always loved. The first chapter dealt with the state when much of it was Indian territory. I read it and thought, I can even add a few things to that. In my jewelry box was a real Indian arrowhead which I had found near the Indian mounds in Moundville before the excavation. I dropped it into my purse and thought, How much I'll have to tell those children!

I spent too much time on the history, and it was late at night before I finished with the other assignments. I almost fell into bed, and there was little time for dreaming. When I did, it was not of my alma mater, nor would it come to mind for many months to come. Not that my determination to go back to college had lessened. It was stronger than ever, but now I must think of the eight children and what I could do for them.

7

My First Full Day of Teaching and Miss Bunker

WHEN MY ALARM WENT OFF NEXT MORNING, I opened my eyes, shut off the ringing alarm, and thought, It's still the middle of the night. I was about to go back to sleep when the thought struck me, Why, this is my first day of teaching!

I crawled reluctantly out of bed and pulled on my robe. Then I hurried to the kitchen to find my father building a fire in the wood range while my mother was slicing the ham by lamplight. Rosa was making biscuits, a new accomplishment of which she was very proud. My mother stopped and looked at me as my eyes were heavy with sleep.

"Aren't you pushing yourself too hard?"

"I am sleepy," I admitted, "but I'm really all right. I know what would wake me up—a cold shower."

"I'll help you in a minute," said my father. He knew I would need water from the well. The shower was a unique affair, one of my funny inventions. Most people made fun of it, but I thought it worked well. We did not have indoor plumbing, and when some of my college friends had visited us in the summer, I, with my father's help, had rigged up the shower. We made it in a closet at the far end of the back porch. My father had built a high shelf by the closet window on which we had placed the large bowl of an old cream separator left over from plantation days. I had then punched holes in a small bucket, which I hung over the spigot to the bowl. My father had built a kind of ladder outside on which one climbed to pour water through the window into the bowl. It held three large buckets. Luckily, the well and pump were close by.

The shower worked if used just right. The idea was to turn on the water long enough to get one's body wet, turn off the water and soap all over, then if one had timed the water right, there should be plenty left to wash off the soap and to rinse a little. If the timing was wrong, one was left standing there full of soap and no water and must yell for help. After being caught in that predicament a few times, I had learned how to manage, and in a few minutes I was back in the kitchen, fresh and hungry.

Breakfast was on the table, my favorite foods: ham cured in my father's smokehouse, eggs, biscuits with butter fresh from the churn, and fig preserves. My mother had made me a lunch of the same.

"Rosa, your biscuits are as good as Mamma's, maybe better." Rosa loved compliments.

"What will you drink with your lunch?" my mother asked.

"Why, I don't know. Daddy, did you see the well there?"

"Yes, and Mr. Douglas mentioned that they mended the well casing. You must not drink from that old well until the water is tested. You must be careful. Old wells often cave in and can be dangerous. You and the children stay away from it until Mr. Douglas assures you it is safe. I'm sure the children's parents will provide water for the school."

To be on the safe side, my mother filled a half-gallon jar of water for us and gave me a sack full of old jelly glasses.

"What would I do without you?" I said tenderly, hugging them all. My father said, "I'll load the car for you while you dress."

When I came out, my father was waiting. "If you will drive me by the store, I'll fill the car with gas."

"I'll pay you back someday."

"Oh stop that," he said, laughing. "Your mother and I only wish we could do more."

I knew how much my father missed farming, but of course he was very grateful to our good friend Mr. Eugene Griffith for giving him the job of running the store to tide him over until he could get back into the work he loved. This was the last store existing in the village. Its days were numbered because the people of Old Spring Hill had begun to go to Demopolis to shop. It was the largest city in Marengo County.

As far back as 1840, when Demopolis was struggling to become a city, Old Spring Hill was a thriving community of many residences and stores, a post office, two doctors' offices, two churches, a grammar school, two academies (male and female), and a large cotton gin. Rich landowners had elected to build their beautiful homes near each other in the village rather than out on their lands, giving Old Spring Hill a unique beauty. When the big plantations went out of existence, the village became smaller and smaller, while Demopolis, located on the Black Warrior River, grew rapidly. Each morning as I followed the little sandy road out of the village, I was reminded that not all of the old beauty was lost. Here and there, peeping from behind the lush pines and blooming crepe myrtle, were the remains of the old antebellum homes, some closed, some in a bad state of decay, a few occupied by descendants of the pioneers. One of them, known as the old Blount home, had been built by my great-great-grandmother.

When we reached the store, I said, "Daddy, I need some pencils and notebook paper. The children are supposed to furnish their supplies, but I doubt if they can. If you will get this, I'll fill the car with gas." My father came back and handed me a sack. "I put an old pencil sharpener in there, too. We have no use for it here. Also, you have a hammer and some nails. Keep the hammer in the car when you are not using it." He glanced at his watch. "You're leaving mighty early."

"I know," I said, "but I have so much to do. Good-bye until this evening." I kissed him and drove off.

Yes, it was early. The sun was just peeping above the tree-tops on the rolling meadows through which I would soon be passing. Now they were a hazy blue in the distance, but I knew that when I got there I would see that they were bright with the last green of summer. The roadsides were colorful, too, with goldenrod, black-eyed susans, and primroses.

The farmers were already at work, some harvesting corn, others baling the last hay of the season. Here the fields were not green but golden, and the odor of newly-mown hay was incredibly sweet. I opened the windshield, as one could with Model T's. I wanted to get the benefit of the air so full of fragrance, familiar to me since childhood.

When I passed through Egypt, I was better prepared than I had been the day before, and I did not let the dear, familiar sights get me down. I just drove straight ahead, looking neither right nor left. As I came in view of the school, the children were there, waiting for me as before. This time the sight of them made my heart glad. Without realizing it, I was beginning to think of them as "my children." Again they were around the car to help the moment it stopped. All wanted to carry the globe.

"Dan," I said, "perhaps you had better carry it. It is very old and might come to pieces. There are many other things to carry in. Minnie, here are watercolors and paper." I was happy to see Minnie's face light up. "There are jelly glasses in one of these sacks. Use one for water because the paints are old and will need soaking."

I had purposely delayed with Minnie until the others had gone in. Then I whispered, "Minnie, you know, don't you, that since school will be in regular session today you won't be able to run to the window and wave when Cluster comes by." The glow went out of Minnie's face as when a cloud passes over the sun. "I'm so sorry," I said, "but you do understand, don't you, and maybe you can explain to Cluster."

"If I ever see him," sighed Minnie. The look on her face tugged at my heartstrings. I didn't see why Minnie couldn't wave if it made her happy. In fact, it might add a little excitement if we all ran to the window and waved. These were quiet, obedient children who seemed to wish only to please, and I did not think they would take advantage of any situation. Then I remembered Reverend Milford's anger, and I guessed I had done the right thing. Turning, I went into the schoolhouse, followed by Minnie. Under a window, I spied an old table.

"Minnie, let's put the things for painting on this table. This will be your paint table, and you may use the stool to sit on. Whenever you have finished with your work, things will be here ready for you to paint pictures." Minnie still looked a little downhearted, but she began to soak the paints. I moved to my desk, and there, among the other things, were the flowers Dan had brought.

"Dan, these are beautiful. I brought a vase. Debra, will you put these flowers in it and use some of the water I brought?

And now will the rest of you girls do something for me? I brought two vases. See all this cotton blooming around us? Cut some of the stalks and make us a pretty bouquet of cotton blooms in the other one."

They laughed, and Dimmie asked, "Cotton in a vase?"

"I know we don't think of cotton as being anything but useful, but it is really pretty. You'll see. Besides, it will soon be gone. If Minnie could paint a picture of it, we'd still have it to enjoy."

The girls took the vase and went out while I went to help Dan and Toby, who were struggling with the large map of Alabama.

"W-W-Where'll we hang it?" asked Dan.

"I think on the wall nearest my desk. As we study Alabama, the map will be handy to point out places."

"Let's hang the Alabama flag on the opposite wall. I guess no one brought in the sack with the hammer and nails."

"I'll get it," said Toby, and he ran to the car.

The girls came in with the vase of cotton blooms. They decided they were pretty after all. I suggested that they set the vase on an unused desk near Minnie's paint table. Minnie became interested but was puzzled.

"How do you paint cotton? It's white and the paper is white?"

"You paint the background around the cotton. I'll show you when I have time." I did not want to tell Minnie that I had studied art because I didn't want to discourage her.

My desk was piled with books. "If we only had some bookshelves," I murmured. "There is some lumber left over from the outhouse."

"I-I think I could do it—if-if Pa would help me," said Dan.

"I know he would," said Debra. "They're picking cotton,

but if you'd show Pa one day, I know he'd get to it soon as he could."

"Now, Dan, if you could put this pencil sharpener on the wall, low enough for Toby to reach, we'll be ready to begin." I handed Toby the box of unsharpened pencils. He was delighted to be given the job.

"Since everyone wants to know about the globe, we'll have a group lesson." The girls helped me arrange the benches in a semicircle around my desk, and I sat on the side nearest the children.

"First, I want to thank all of you for being so helpful. Did you see how well Dan and Toby hung the map, the flag, and the pencil sharpener for us?" Toby beamed, and Dan hung his head with embarrassed pleasure. It was still early, but the children were anxious to begin and so was I. I reached for the globe and was about to speak when a car drove into the yard. It was Miss Bunker who now came up the steps, her arms loaded with books. She sat on the back bench and motioned to me to go on with what I was doing. I tried, but I had lost the children's attention. They were twisting and turning, trying to see who was sitting in the back of their school.

"Boys and girls," I said. "Let me introduce you to Miss Bunker. She helps all the schools in the county, and she will help us." Miss Bunker waved, and some of them waved back. Then the children were satisfied, and I looked into eight eager faces. How lucky I was to have the opportunity to teach such wonderful children. But could I do it? Reverend Milford's words came back to me: "If you can't teach 'em, you don't b'long here."

Well, now would be the test, and Miss Bunker was here to see. For a moment I was back at my alma mater a year ago, trying out for the dramatic club. Now I had another performance to give, only this one was even more exciting. I took the globe in my lap. The children leaned forward. One could have heard a pin drop.

"Yesterday," I said, "when I told you I was going to bring a globe, you did not know what a globe was. Then I told you what it represents. Does anyone remember?" Several hands went up.

"Minnie, can you tell us?"

"I think—I think you said the world."

"You are right. Minnie, you have a good memory. This is a small replica of our world."

"Round like that?" asked Toby.

"Yes, Toby. Exactly."

"Then why don't we fall off?"

"Toby, when Columbus and other explorers sailed around the world and proved it was round, many people asked that question. You see, at first everyone thought the world was flat, just like this desk. They thought that if a person got in a ship and sailed far enough, he'd come to the end and fall off. When Columbus decided to go sailing to discover new places, can't you hear the people saying to him, 'Better look out, Columbus, you'll fall off!' But he did not think so. Can anyone tell us why we don't fall off?" Debra held up her hand.

"Yes, Debra?"

"Well, it's something that holds us and everything to the earth. It's called grav—— grav——."

"Yes, gravity," I said, and wrote the word on the board and pronounced it. "Let's say it together."

"Now we'll prove that gravity holds us to the earth. Let's all stand up."

They looked puzzled, but they stood. "Now let's all jump." I began to jump. At first some were timid, but finally all were jumping so much that the floor began to shake. I decided we had better stop before it fell in. All sat down, out of breath and laughing.

"Well," I said, "what happened when we jumped up in the air?"

"We came back down," laughed Debra, not waiting to hold up her hand.

"Toby," I said, "do you play ball?"

"Yes ma'am, I like to play ball."

"When you throw your ball in the air, does it stay up there?"

"No ma'am, it comes back down."

"I'll tell you a little story," I began, and was going to tell them about Sir Isaac Newton, who discovered the law of gravity, but before I could say more, there was the familiar rumbling on the road. All eyes were turned toward the window except Minnie's. She sat as rigid as a statue with her eyes closed. I thought if I lived to be a hundred, I would never forget the misery written on that face. It was hard for me to understand such unhappiness in a family when in my own there had always been so much love and understanding.

I felt that the older children understood because they were now looking at Minnie with something like pity. The logging truck passed out of hearing, and I felt that the crisis had passed, but it was not forgotten. This did not seem to be the right time to continue the lesson; therefore, I said, "Children, I need to talk with Miss Bunker. You may go out and play for a little while, and Toby, here is a ball if you wish to play catch. Go out as I introduce you to Miss Bunker, and maybe you'd like to speak to her as you go." I called their names by grades but did not call Minnie because I had a feeling she would prefer not to go out just yet.

"Minnie, would you like to meet Miss Bunker?"

"No ma'am—not right now."

"Then why don't you try the paints and see how they are doing."

"Yes'm, I'll do that."

Miss Bunker, looking rather puzzled, joined me. There was a bench in the back of the room out of Minnie's hearing, and I suggested that we sit there. I hated for Minnie to know that she was the subject of our conversation, but her back was turned to us and she seemed engrossed with the paints.

"You really had those children with you," said Miss Bunker. "Then what in the world happened?"

I felt that Miss Bunker could understand the situation only if she knew the whole story; therefore, I told her all.

"So she is really serious about this young man?"

"Oh, she's serious all right."

"I'm sorry you had to open with such a harrowing experience, but I doubt if anyone could have handled it any better. What is your relationship with Minnie?"

"We're good friends. She is not interested in books, but she loves painting. I think I can reach her that way."

"As a whole, how is the eighth grade comprehension?"

"Oh, they don't have that." I stopped short. Then the meaning of the word came to me, and I looked at Miss Bunker, whose eyes were brimming pools of laughter. I blushed, and then I laughed too. "Well, maybe they don't, at that, only Debra. She is a real student and will, I think, go places. Her brother Dan is behind because of helping his father and missing school. He has difficulty talking, but he is much brighter than he appears. He has good ideas and already is a great help to me. Dimmie is very bright, and I've told you about Minnie. She is bright enough if I could only get her interested."

"Susie," said Miss Bunker, "did you ever hear the saying that teachers are born, not made? Well, I think maybe you were born to be one."

"Oh," I said. "You think so?"

"Yes. I enjoyed watching you, and I wish I could stay and hear what you do the rest of the day. Of course, you don't have any teaching experience and you are bound to make many mistakes, but you're going to make it all right. At first, I worried about you but not anymore. Now get Toby and we'll have the reading demonstration because I do need to go."

I called him and said, "Toby, Miss Bunker is going to help us with reading. Won't that be fun?" He did not seem so sure, but he soon warmed up to her. She turned to the first lesson. It was about two children and their dog. She asked Toby questions about them. I could see that Miss Bunker was establishing a background of interest. When she felt he was ready to read, she pulled a tongue depresser out of her pocket and put it under the first line.

"Toby," said Miss Bunker, "when you first learn to read, hold a marker under the line. That is much better than pointing with your finger. I'll give you this, but a folded piece of paper would do." She developed the story line by line and then played games, asking him to find certain lines. Last, she pulled flash cards with the words in the story out of her pocket. "Here are some blank cards for you, Susie, and a large ink pen for printing. Flash cards are a follow-up. Toby, I'll be back next week and you can show me what you have learned."

"Yes, ma'am," he said. He was so proud of his accomplishment that he was still clutching the preprimer.

"Susie, here are the textbooks I found," said Miss Bunker, pointing to the stack she had left on the bench when she first came. "There is a full set of the eighth grade books and a few others. I'll keep looking."

"The price," I began, but Miss Bunker waved that aside. "These are a gift," she said. "Now good-bye until next week." The children and I stood on the porch and watched her go. I felt a sense of loss. Now I was really on my own.

8

We Have a Pet

MISS BUNKER DID NOT GET BACK THE NEXT WEEK or the next. I began to worry about her. I called a number she had given me, just to inquire, and was told that she had been called away because of illness in her family. She would probably be gone another week.

I was pleased with the progress of some of my pupils, although I would have liked Miss Bunker's approval on certain matters. For one thing, as Mr. Dick had said, there were too many grades for one teacher. During the first few days, I had tried to solve this problem by staying until four o'clock. The children were willing, but some of the parents had complained, saying this was one of the busiest times of the year with cotton to be picked and they preferred that the children get out at the regular time, which was three o'clock.

I tried to solve the problem another way. Dimmie, the Milford in seventh grade, was unusually bright, and I combined some of her subjects with the eighth grade. The eighth grade

Alabama history was so interesting to all the children that often I made it a group lesson. Even Toby loved the part about early Alabama and the Indians, and they all enjoyed my stories about going to school in the little town of Moundville, where the Indian mounds were located. I told how the state had excavated the mounds, finding many relics. I showed the arrowhead I had found behind the mounds before the excavation.

Toby Douglas was making rapid progress in everything, especially reading. He had completed two preprimers. Whenever he finished one, he was allowed to take it home and read to his parents, who were so pleased that they stopped by the school to thank me. While visiting the school, Toby's father explained about the well.

"It was not safe," Mr. Douglas said, "so we covered it, but when we finish picking cotton, we men will get together and fix it. Until then maybe it would be best that each of you bring water to drink, as you have been doing."

I had found a large piece of paneling, and Dan helped me nail it on the wall for a bulletin board. When one of the children did an especially neat paper, I tacked it up for all to see. Although Dan had trouble with other subjects, he was my most advanced math student. He was very proud to see two of his papers on the bulletin board.

Cluster still passed daily, and there was always the same tension in the air; we just did not speak of it. I wondered how Minnie felt, but I did not ask. She buried herself in her efforts at painting. I cut mats for her best pictures, and we tacked them around to brighten up the room. Minnie now seemed to be making a greater effort to do her schoolwork, and I praised her for that.

The lazy, warm days of September passed, and the brisk

October weather took over. The owners of the field surrounding the school had gone over it twice, picking the cotton, and now instead of the soft, white blooms, there were only harsh ugly stalks. But the changing leaves colored the surrounding trees and more than made up for the loss in beauty. One day I called Minnie to the porch.

"Look at those beautiful trees so red and gold against that azure sky—and the white clouds flying. I'll bet you could make a lovely painting of that scene." Minnie immediately got to work and did her best painting.

"Minnie," I said, "if you'd like, I'll take the painting home and mat it, then frame it if I can find a frame that will do. I saw some old ones in our attic. Then I'll bring it back so that you can show it to your parents."

Minnie was very pleased and set about doing other paintings of the autumn foliage.

Dan was distressed because his mother's flowers were gone, but when he learned how I loved the bright, colored leaves, he brought some in each day. The other children caught the idea, and soon the room was a riot of color. For the first time, these children became aware of the beauty of the seasons and how to express their feelings by using the gifts of nature.

One day Dan brought something very interesting. It was a branch from a chinquapin tree. It had many clusters of the burrs, and all were filled with ripe chinquapins. The class got pliers and pulled the chinquapins out and ate them. They tasted like chestnuts, only sweeter.

"I have not seen one of these trees since I was a child," I said. "I would love to see it."

"It's not so far," said Debra. "We could walk there at noon. You can't get there in a car."

"I have an idea," I said. "If all of us could bring lunches tomorrow, we could start our lessons early and eat early, too, then go for a nature walk at noon. Autumn is such a beautiful time, and I have been hoping to do that. How far is the chinquapin tree?"

"N-n-not so far," said Dan.

In the meantime, the weather had turned a little cooler, and we decided to try out our heater to see how well it heated the room. From time to time the children's fathers had brought wood, which now made a high stack in the backyard, and they had put bundles of fat pine under the house for kindling. The girls helped Dan bring in wood and kindling, and I furnished an old newspaper.

"Oh," said Debra, "we forgot matches."

"My father remembered," I said. I reached in the drawer and pulled out a big box of matches. "Don't make a very big fire because these heaters can really roast a person."

They pulled benches around the heater and were sitting there cozy and busy, some studying, some doing assignments, and one class having a lesson with me. Suddenly I whispered, "Sh-h-h-h," and put my finger over my lips. Then I pointed to a rafter overhead. There sat a little mouse looking at us with beady black eyes.

"W-w-want me to kill it?" asked Dan.

"Why, no. In homes, you have to destroy them because they do damage, but I don't see how it can do any harm here. It is probably hungry, poor little thing." I reached for my lunch and broke off a crust of bread from a sandwich. "Dan, if you can reach the top of that rafter, crumble this in front of the mouse. Be very quiet because it may not trust us yet." After Dan did as I asked, he sat back down and all waited, watching the mouse. It sat very still for a little while, then crept slowly to the crumbs. It then ate ravenously as if it were starved. When finished, it looked around for more.

"Want to give it more?" Dan asked.

"Let's wait awhile. I think it will stay around. I wish we had something small enough to give it water."

"A jelly glass?" asked Minnie.

"That's too big," I said. "But I have an idea. Minnie, let me have the glass of water that's on your paint table. Now I'll get another piece of bread. We'll soak it in the water. If the little thing is famished for water, this will help." Dan put the bread, dripping water, in the same place. Again the mouse ate ravenously. Soon it seemed satisfied. It sat on its haunches and washed its face, very much as a cat does. The children were so amused that they had to cover their mouths to keep from laughing out loud and scaring the little animal away. My dear little Cammie was shaking with laughter, but she managed to control it.

"Well, children," I said, "I think we have ourselves a pet."

9

Our Nature Walk

THE DAY FOR OUR NATURE WALK DAWNED BRIGHT and blue and a little warmer but typical October weather for Alabama. It was perfect for our walk. The children applied themselves diligently to get most lessons done before lunch. When it was almost twelve, they ate hurriedly. I put on my old tennis shoes for walking. We remembered to leave food for the mouse.

"Shall we lock the door?" asked Dan.

"I think not," I said. "Just close it because we won't be gone that long." The only way I could lock my car was to take out the key. Early Model T's had no glass windows but instead had isinglass curtains, which one could put up in case of rain or cold weather.

Dan and Debra led the way. The going was rough at first because we had to cross cotton rows for quite a distance before coming to the woods. When we reached them, I was in no hurry because beauty was all about. I wished I knew more about the flora, but there were trees I recognized. The hickories were a glowing yellow. "Aren't these trees beautiful?" I said. "I believe they are all loaded with nuts."

"Move back, everybody," said Dan, and he shook a limb. Nuts aplenty fell.

"Look," I said, "we are robbing somebody." I pointed to two squirrels peeping through the foliage. The children filled their pockets with nuts, and there were plenty left for the squirrels.

The buckeye bushes were a bright orange in color and loaded with buckeyes. Toby started to pick them.

"Wait, Toby," I said. "I'm not sure but I think I've heard that buckeyes are poisonous. Just get some of the pretty branches to brighten up our room."

Then Toby's keen eyes spied an object on one of the branches. "Miss Susie, what is this?"

"Why, that is a cocoon. If we keep it until spring, perhaps we'll see a butterfly or a moth come out. Handle it carefully." Then we walked on until Dan held up his hand for all to stop.

"What is it?" I whispered, fearing he had seen a snake. We looked where Dan pointed. At first, we saw nothing, but soon we became aware that a huge hoot owl was perched on a limb blinking down at us. We stood very still for a while, watching fascinated. Then I looked at my watch and decided we had better move on. After a good bit more walking, Dan pointed.

"There it is, the chinquapin tree." But between us and the tree was a little creek.

"How do you get across?" I asked.

"A little farther along there is a log," said Debra. "Have you ever walked a log, Miss Susie?"

"Oh, yes, but it has been a long time." To the children, walking a log was nothing, but they were concerned about their teacher. Dan got in front and held my hand. Some of the older girls held my other hand from the rear. The only problem was that the log slanted downhill. It was round and slippery, but we made it across.

Chinquapin trees, as I remembered, were amazing. At this time of year they were loaded with sticky clusters full of ripe chinquapins. We had brought two big sacks, which we filled so quickly that we wished we had brought more. The burrs were too sticky to carry by hand.

"Well, children," I said, looking at my watch, "it's a quarter after one. We'd better get back as soon as possible." We started to cross the log in the same method as before, but just as I stepped on it, a big snake slithered from under it and began to swim in spirals and then, luckily for us, swam on down the creek. I was trying so hard to determine if it could be a cottonmouth that I missed my footing and went into the water knee-deep. Toby tried to grab me, and in he went up to his neck. The soft mud oozed into my shoes and stockings, and getting out was not easy, even with all trying to help. When I did make it, I was muddy up to my knees. When Dan finally got Toby out, Toby was muddy all over. Dan gallantly pulled off his shirt and tried to wipe us off.

"We'd better walk back in a hurry. That will help us get dry and warm, Toby. He was still clutching the pretty sprays and the cocoon. When we came in sight of the schoolhouse, I almost dropped in my tracks. There in the yard was Miss Bunker's car and with her was the superintendent, Mr. Killingsworth. Both were walking about on the porch.

"Oh, God," I prayed, "help us!"

Dan said, "An-An me without no shirt!"

Toby saved the day. When he saw Miss Bunker, the kind lady who started him off in reading, he ran ahead and clasped her hand.

"We've been on a nature walk," he panted, "and see what I

found?" He showed her the cocoon. "But we done our lessons first. We started work at seven this morning. You ain't mad at us, are you?"

"Of course not," laughed Miss Bunker. By that time all of the children were there, and I was bringing up the rear. I introduced each pupil to Mr. Killingsworth.

"Susie," he said with a laugh, "I see you are as full of enthusiasm as ever."

"And of mud," I laughed. Then we all talked at once, trying to relate our exciting adventure. But words were not necessary. One look at Toby and me told the tale. I whispered to Dan to show the chinquapins so he dumped the contents of the sacks on the porch.

"What are they?" asked Miss Bunker. Mr. Killingsworth did not know either.

"Dan," I said, "will you get the pliers out of my tool box? We'll give our guests a treat." In a few minutes they were all eating chinquapins.

"What are they, little chestnuts?"

"They are called chinquapins, but they are little wild chestnuts. I'm told that they are almost extinct. Dan found this tree. Each of you take some home with you."

"Susie, we have been looking at what you have done inside," Mr. Killingsworth told me, "and you have worked wonders with this place and such good work on the bulletin board."

"Most of the credit goes to the children," I protested.

"I have never seen inside before," he said. "I did not know the room had no ceiling. Will you be warm this winter?"

"Don't worry," I said, "that heater works wonders. We tried it out for a little while yesterday."

"There is some money allotted for fuel," he continued. "I'll see that you get a ton of coal. By putting a few shovels on after you build the fire, it will last a long time without your continually feeding it wood. By the way, do you have to build the fires yourself?"

"Well, sir, I could, but Dan seems very good at it."

He called me aside. "Do you think Dan would accept a little something for his work, say, five dollars a month?"

"I wish he would," I said, "but let me handle it. He would not want to be treated as a janitor."

"Of course not. I'll leave it to you."

Toby had gotten his preprimer and was waiting to read from it. He was just beginning on his third preprimer. Miss Bunker could not believe he had gone so far. He got his marker. "See," he said, "I did not forget." He read a page, then Miss Bunker took the marker away. "Now," she said, "Hold your book with both hands. Look at each line before you read and read the whole page to me." Toby did as she bade, and Miss Bunker hugged him.

"Toby, I am so proud of you. You read just as you talk. And I'm proud of this whole school." Then she turned to the other children. "I'm anxious to see what you are learning, too. Your work on the bulletin board is so good. I'll be back soon. Today we have to visit many schools."

I noticed the superintendent walking around the building. He was inspecting the structure with a frown. I could not be sure, of course, but I had a feeling that he was going to use his influence to see that these people got their graveled road so the children could ride the school bus.

After our visitors left, the children and I could not get down to ordinary lessons because so much had happened. But I had an idea. "I think it would be nice if each of you could write a story about our nature walk. Don't discuss it with anyone else because I want it to be in your own words. I can help you with the spelling or you can use the dictionary. Toby, you and I will sit on that back bench and I'll help you. Lily, do what you can by yourself, and I'll help you if you need it."

Minnie held up her hand. "Could I just paint a picture of it?"

"Well, yes, but I would like you to write a story, too, because you need that experience. It doesn't have to be long."

Silence filled the room, but it was a happy silence with much going on. The day had turned out even better than I had expected.

10

Minnie's Love Affair

BACK AT HOME THAT EVENING, I FOUND IN THE ATTIC just the right frame for Minnie's painting. Then I matted it with the best poster board I had. When I showed the painting to my parents, they said, "Are you sure you did not do some of it?"

"I did not touch it," I said. "All I did was to call this girl's attention to the pretty view."

Next day at school Minnie could hardly believe how much better her painting looked matted and framed.

"This picture is a little heavy with the glass, frame, and all," I said. "When school is out, suppose I drive you home. I'm anxious to meet your mother anyway." I was also secretly hoping that Minnie's pretty artwork would help improve her relations with her father.

The first lesson of the day was a group lesson. I had taken the children's stories home and read them carefully. They were very revealing, not only about their own abilities but about their personalities. Now I wanted each to read his or her own

story aloud. I wanted them to learn to give impartial construc-
tive criticism, both about their own work and about that of
the others.

Toby was learning to print very well, but he was not yet up
to composing a story on his own. Therefore, I had written it
for him as he dictated. Then he had signed his name.

Before the day was over, he would learn to read it so he
could do so for his parents when he got home. But now I read
it aloud for him:

> We went for a walk. Miss Susie wanted to see the chin-
> quapin tree. We had to walk a log over the creek and Miss
> Susie saw a snake and she fell in and I fell in and the snake
> was big. The snake wanted to bite us but it didn't.
> Toby Douglas

Lily had written a similar story, also centered around the
snake and the log accident. I corrected the spelling, and then,
with my help, Lily was able to read it. She, too, was proud of
her story and worked on it during the day so she could read it
to her parents.

All of the stories had the same theme except Dan's. He
mentioned the snake and told about our falling in the creek,
but his main theme was the pretty autumn woods, the hickory
trees with nuts, the squirrels, and the owl.

Dan's was the only story that had captured the aesthetic
side. Perhaps he could put on paper what he could not put
into words because of his speech difficulty. I sat and looked at
them all. I knew them better now.

"Children," I said, "I am very proud of you. You had an
experience and, in your own words, you have put it down on
paper."

All were enthusiastic, and when they went home each had a story to share with parents.

When I went with the Milford children to their home after school, we found Reverend and Mrs. Milford under the trees cleaning fish they had caught. Minnie introduced me to her mother and to her two little brothers.

"I been wanting to meet you, Miss Susie," said Mrs. Milford, wiping her hands on her apron. Reverend Milford did not look up.

I spoke to him pleasantly, and he did not answer but walked away. Mrs. Milford tried to ignore his rudeness.

"Oh," I said, examining the fish, "these are beautiful fish. Did you catch them?" They had caught them in the very creek I had fallen into.

"Minnie, show them your painting." The mother was fascinated.

"Minnie did that!" she exclaimed.

"Every bit of it," I said.

Then Reverend Milford came and looked. Mrs. Milford said, "Why, our Minnie paints pictures like a real artist, don't she?"

"Indeed she does," I said. "And I hope Minnie will enter it in the county fair."

"I will," said Minnie, happiness showing in her face.

"You been so good to our young un's," Mrs. Milford said. "Teaching our Minnie to paint and sending us all them textbooks. Don't we owe you some'n?"

"No, ma'am, they were given to me by the supervisor. They were a gift for the children."

"Is Minnie doin' better 'bout that boy, Miss Susie?" she asked.

I felt I had to be honest. "Mrs. Milford, I really don't know. She buries herself in her painting, but sometimes she gets a faraway expression on her face as if she does not even know where she is. She never mentions his name to me."

"She don't to me neither. I hope she's getting over him. How the other chillun doin'?"

"They are doing very well, and Dimmie is a real student. Both Cammie and Lily are doing better. But our supervisor says most of the children are not up to grade level."

"Miss Susie, you're the only teacher has stuck to the school and worked with our young uns. We hope you won't leave before the year is out as most teachers done."

"I'll surely be here all the school year, the Lord being willing."

"Won't you come in and set a spell?" invited Mrs. Milford.

"Thank you," I said. "Let me come another time. I have so much to do with all these lessons to prepare. Would you like to keep Minnie's painting for a while?"

"We shore would," said Mrs. Milford. "Now wait, Miss Susie. We got more fish than we need. Let me give you a mess."

"We really like fresh fish. But you have so many in your family. Are you sure you can spare them?"

She waved my remarks aside and got a sack to put the fish in.

"They are all cleaned and ready to cook," she said.

"Thank you so much. That will be a real treat. Now good-bye until tomorrow." I left feeling I had made a friend in Mrs. Milford, but Reverend Milford was as difficult as ever.

It was almost November, and yet the day had became un-seasonably warm. The sky in the west was very dark, and I could hear the rumbling of thunder. When I was halfway home, the rain began to fall. I quickly got out and put chains on the rear tires, something I had done many, many times. The sky was looking more ominous, and I did not bother to put up curtains because that took time. I just wanted to get home.

These little roads through the Black Belt had another aggravating quality besides the deep bogginess of winter. Under summer suns, they become hard like concrete, and when the first big rain came to soften the top layer of soil, they could be as slick as glass. With chains, people who knew these roads and had developed a certain skill could generally get where they wanted to go. There had been little rain in this section, and I realized I was facing this all-too-well-known situation today. The ditches on either side were not deep. If the car slid into one, however, there was nothing to do but sit there until help came along. One old fellow made money when conditions were right for these problems by going up and down the roads with a team of mules to pull the unfortunate people out. My father got stuck in a ditch once, and after that he would never take the car on slick roads unless my sister or I drove for him. Usually it was fun for me to drive under these conditions, but I could not risk getting stuck today because I had too much to do so I did all the right things, and these things were, besides putting on chains, keeping the car in high gear as much as possible, going at a moderate rate of speed, and never using brakes or low gear unless absolutely necessary. These were the Black-Belt rules of the road.

The car skidded a lot, and keeping it on the road was hard work because there was no automatic steering in those days, and when finally I reached the sandy road of Old Spring Hill, I was out of breath, but home was only half a mile away.

When at last I drove into the little shed that my father had built next to the back porch, I cut off the engine and laid my head on the steering wheel to recover.

My younger sister Elizabeth was already home from school and came running with an umbrella.

"I don't need it," I said. "I am already wet. But here—take this sack of fresh fish for supper. They are all cleaned and filleted."

"Where did you get them?"

"Mrs. Milford gave them to me."

"But—but—I thought Reverend Milford didn't like you."

"Oh, he doesn't. Mrs. Milford gave them to me. Maybe his attitude will change someday." I started the motor and backed out. I had to laugh at my sister, still standing in the rain, her faced filled with amazement. She could not get used to my many surprises.

"Get in the house out of this sharp lightning," I yelled to her. "I'm going to the store to see if Dad is ready to come home."

My father did not usually close the store this early, but when he saw my wet clothes, he decided that we had better get home so I helped him lock up. On the way home, he said, "It's just as well that we closed because I doubt if anyone would come out in this weather to trade."

By the time I had changed into dry clothes and washed my hair, supper was ready. I went to the table to find a large platter of delectable fried fish and some of my mother's special hush puppies as an accompaniment. My parents reminded me several times to tell Mrs. Milford what a treat the fresh fish were to us all.

The wet weather continued through Thursday, but by the end of the week the sun was shining again. On Friday night after supper, I said to my father, "Daddy use some of your best weather predictions and tell me what the weather will be like tomorrow."

"Well, I think we'll have a pretty day. When I went to the well for water just now, the rain had stopped. There was blue sky showing and in the west the sun was setting clear."

"Now what are you up to?" asked my mother, jokingly.

"I was going to ask you, Mamma, if you'll be using Dan and the buggy Saturday. I would like to go to Egypt and if I go in the buggy, I can take the food you want to send to the old people."

"I had not planned to go anywhere."

"You know I have not been back to Egypt since we moved. I want to spend the whole day there. I have been thinking of doing that one Saturday. Autumn is a pretty time to go, and I doubt if we'll have much more weather like this."

My father looked very serious and a little worried. "I'm sure you'll be all right, but I do hate for you to go alone. The plantation is so deserted now."

"I'll go with you, Tutter," said Elizabeth. (Tutter is what my sisters called me.)

"I wish you would, but I'd better warn you, Elizabeth. I'm going to take my saddle and ride Dan to all my favorite places when I get there. Think you could ride behind me as you did when you were a little girl?"

"Uh-huh—I guess so," she said, making a grimace. She was never the enthusiastic rider that I was. My father got up from the table and said with a smile: "I can see that Dan is in for a big day. I'd better go and give him an extra feeding of oats."

11

A Day on Egypt

GOING TO EGYPT BY BUGGY WAS LIKE OLD TIMES. Even if we could have gotten there by car, which I doubted because the new owners did not keep up the plantation road, by going this way, I would have Dan to ride when I got there. Dan was an old horse now, but when we turned into the road leading to Egypt, he trotted along briskly, apparently feeling that he, too, was going home. The sun was well up, yet we traveled in shade provided by the living fence of mock-orange trees that bordered the road.

When we neared the gate where we would turn into the plantation road, I whispered to Elizabeth, "Let's see if Dan remembers." I gave him the reins, and he did all the right things, slowed to a walk and turned correctly, but I think he was surprised at what lay before him. Actually, it could hardly be called a road—just deep, winding ruts that led a mile to the main house and surrounding buildings. We followed the tracks slowly and looked for things no longer there. In place of the waving hay fields and the lush crops, we found weeds. The cabins whose friendly occupants used to wave to us were empty now, with many broken windows and crumbling chimneys. When we came to Jolly Bottom, that rich strip of bottomland that lay on each side of the big creek that flowed through Egypt, we were relieved to find the bridge in good repair. Here Dan resumed his usual trot until he reached the other side. The sound of his crossing had such a familiar ring that it brought back very endearing memories. When I became old enough to go horseback riding in the afternoons with friends, my mother used to say, "When I hear your horses crossing the bridge, I know you are only five minutes away and that it's time to put supper on the table." These friends had a standing invitation to stay for supper, which they often did. My mother was correct about "five minutes," because after the crossing, we would race at full gallop until we reached the house. Now, with Dan struggling to pull the buggy over what had been the road, it took a great deal longer.

In a way, I was prepared for the changes that now existed. I had been told about the fire at the plantation home and what to expect, but somehow I was not ready at all for what greeted me when we drove into what once was the front yard. True, two rooms and a portion of the back porch were still standing, but everything had a black, charred appearance. What hurt most, I think, was the absence of the beautiful shade trees under which we played as children. In their place were piles of charred planks and other debris. There was no smokehouse in the backyard, no henhouse, no outhouse back of the garden— in fact, no fence to show even where the garden once was—no front gate, nothing. But when I planned this day, I had promised myself that I was not going back to grieve over what had been but to visit beloved spots and to relive that life through memories. Elizabeth, however, did understand how hard it was to see the home place in ruins and she said, "Tutter, I knew it would hurt."

I decided to get out and walk around, but when I invited Elizabeth, she declined, saying she had already seen everything and that anyway she needed to study for upcoming tests. I climbed down from the buggy to get a better view.

"I'm glad to see the windmill still pumping water and the concrete drinking trough still intact," I said to Elizabeth. She began to snicker. I knew why, and I laughed with her.

"I know what you are thinking about. When you were little and our cousins your age came for a visit, if our father were not around, you'd strip to your underwear and go wading in the trough, stirring up the moss so badly that the stock would not drink."

"Look at Dan," I interrupted myself to say, "I believe he remembers the trough and seems to want a drink now." He was tugging at the reins and trying to get to the water. Elizabeth let him go, and he hurried over to refresh himself. I took the carton of drinks out of the buggy and set it down in the water to get cool. Then I wandered over to the building that had served as a commissary. The door was unlocked so I peeped in to see only a few bales of rotting hay and some empty barrels. The shelves were still intact on the walls, and so was the counter where there once had been a cash register. My mind wandered back to the days when every space was filled with produce. I especially remembered the boxes of lemon and peppermint stick candy for which I saved my pennies.

When Dan finished drinking, Elizabeth drove over to the commissary building where I stood, deep in reverie.

"Elizabeth, I was thinking of Saturday mornings here when

the day laborers came for their week's wages, fifty cents a day, as I remember, three pounds of side meat, a peck of meal, and a half gallon of sorghum molasses."

"That doesn't seem very much for a week's work," reflected Elizabeth.

"Those wages do seem small," I agreed, "especially compared to present-day ones. But you could buy things so cheaply then—a loaf of bread for a dime." I looked above the door and exclaimed with surprise, "Why, the old bell is still up there!" It was a small, rusty bell with a string to pull. "Remember, if someone needed something, they would ring this bell. Only our parents and Uncle Reuben carried the keys."

"This was not the main plantation bell was it?" she asked.

"Oh, no—the main bell was much larger." I walked to what was once the corner of the yard, where the bell frame still stood. "The bell hung here, one with a beautiful tone. Don't you remember? Daddy rang it at daybreak on weekdays and it could be heard all over the plantation."

"Do we still have it?" she asked, but I did not hear her. My mind had traveled back to the time when I could faintly hear the bell in my sleep, followed by the jingling of harnesses as hands went forth to the fields, sounds that I hoped I could keep forever in my memory because to me they heralded the beginning of a new and exciting day on Egypt. I looked at Elizabeth. I thought she had said something.

"I'm sorry. My mind was far away."

"I said, do we still have the bell?"

"No, I wish we did. Daddy said he had so much to think about when we moved that he forgot the bell. When he sent for it, it was gone. We never found a clue."

"You said Daddy rang the bell at daylight. Did we have breakfast so early?"

"Oh, no. Daddy visited all the work areas first and would come home for a big breakfast about eight o'clock. The black women took breakfast, always in tin buckets, to their men in the fields at about the same time. I was often there on my horse when they ate."

"What did they eat for breakfast?"

"Always the same thing, hot corn bread (or sometimes what they called flour bread), long slices of side meat, fried brown, and in the bottom of the bucket, molasses with some of the bacon grease poured in. This they sopped clean with the bread, and it all looked very good. Sometimes there was a hot yam that had been roasted in the ashes, and they often brought one for me. All of the cabins where they lived had fireplaces for cooking. With breakfast, they drank a bottle of buttermilk. Then each man would pull a little cloth bag of tobacco out of his pocket and roll a cigarette, which he smoked leisurely as he sat on the plow stock, that is, if plowing was what he was doing."

I climbed back in the buggy and took the reins.

"Let's drive up to the big barn; I'm glad to see it is still standing. It was well built. Remember, our Uncle Charlie, a really good builder, came from Mississippi to do the job. It took all winter. People came from miles around to see it—the largest barn ever built around here."

"I still hear people talk about it," she said. The big doors were open, and we drove right in. Some tin was off the roof, letting in shafts of light which showed that the heavy beams were still solid.

"Look," I said in amazement. "Some of the stalls still have the mules' names over them. You were too little to remember this, but when I was a small child, it amused people that I knew every mule's name, some sixty in number, and also their personalities."

"You and I enjoyed different things about plantation life," she said.

"Oh, I loved everything that went on here, but I loved the great out-of-doors. Before I got a horse of my own, I would meet the hands at the big gate at sundown to be lifted to a sweaty mule's back. I got a big thrill out of riding to the barn. When I came in to supper, with mule's hair stuck to my legs, Mamma would smile and hand me a bar of soap. No words were necessary because this was a common occurrence. There was a big zinc tub of water in a closet at the end of the back porch nearest the pump. There were clean clothes on a low shelf for me and for you, too—only I was generally the culprit who brought in all the plantation dirt." We laughed together as we turned around and started back. Then I saw something that sobered me up. We had reached a place where we got a full view of the area where the many cabins had been located a short distance back of the main house. I was shocked to see that very few remained.

"What happened to the quarters?" I asked.

"The quarters?" she repeated. "I don't know."

"You remember, all the cabins where the day laborers lived? It was called the quarters. I see very few left. I can remember when the hands numbered a hundred and more."

"We could ask Uncle Reuben, I guess."

"I have fond memories of those quarters," I told her. "On summer nights we'd sit on our front gallery and listen to the occupants sing all the pretty old spirituals such as 'Go down, Moses,' 'Come, Mary, Toll the Bell,' 'Climbing Jacob's Ladder,' and others. Sometimes, when we had company, they would come up to the house to sing for us. Our mother would make a big freezer of ice cream to serve everyone. It's hard to believe that so much beauty is gone. I remember how the far-off call of the whip-o-wills blended so perfectly with the singing on those summer nights."

We drove down the hill to where the two cabins stood. They were more like institutions, having had so many additions through the years, for horses, cows, chickens, ducks, geese, and the like. Uncle Cajer even once had what he called his store, about the size of a large closet, at one end of the porch. He knew nothing of buying wholesale and selling retail, but if he paid ten cents for a box of gingersnaps, he sawed the box in half and sold each part for a dime, so he made money. Mammy Lou contributed her share through her midwifery and herb garden. It was a standing joke among the black people that this old couple had what they called "rusty dollars" hidden away and could afford to buy a horse or cow when the plantation couldn't.

"Bur, you never knew this, but one day, by accident, I happened to see their hiding place. Our mother needed a special herb for cooking and sent me to get it from Mammy Lou. As I stepped up on the porch, I could see both her and Uncle Cajer down on their knees doing something, praying, I first thought, so I stopped and was very quiet. Then I saw that they were counting coins and dropping them into a long stocking. I knew I was not supposed to see this so I cleared my throat and called, 'Mammy Lou.' They quickly dropped the stocking through a hole in the floor and put the plank back in place. Then Mammy Lou came to the door and said, 'Come in chile. You come to see us?'

"I explained my errand and she went to get the herb. Uncle Cajer hobbled over to me on his cane.

"'Mis Susie, you ever seed any goslin's?' Maybe he wanted to get my mind off what I saw.

"'What are goslin's, Uncle Cajer?'

"'They's little geese, chile. Lemme git some cawn an' call 'em.'

"While he was doing this, Mammy Lou returned with the herbs. I was fascinated with the goslings that had gathered for the corn, so I lingered to watch.

"'Don' let dat gander git you,' cautioned Mammy Lou. 'He'll whup you wid his wings and he kin hurt.' They both went back in the house and I heard Mammy Lou ask Uncle Cajer, 'Reckon dat chile seed whut we wuz doin'?'

"'Naw,' Uncle Cajer reassured her. 'She didn' know.'

"I did, though, and told our mother about it as soon as I got back to the house. She looked very serious and called me aside.

"'It's very important that you never, never tell what you saw—not to anyone.'

"'Why?' I asked.

"'Well,' she reflected, 'I don't know of anyone on the plantation who might harm those old people, but if word got around about their money and the hiding place, somebody just might.'

"I promised, and over all those years I never did.

"Well, here we are."

We pulled over under the mulberry trees that shaded the yard. Mammy Lou came hurrying out, and Uncle Reuben came from his cabin across the little drive.

"My chillun done come to see us," exclaimed Mammy Lou, hugging us. Uncle Reuben, shaking our hands heartily, seemed equally glad to see us. Aunt Deanna, sitting on their porch and quilting as usual, waved, and we waved back.

"Deanna don't feel so good, but she wants y'all to come see her fo' you leaves."

"We will," we both assured him. "And where is Uncle Cajer?" I asked, looking around the place. I half expected him to be there, doing some chore.

"Honey, Cage been in de bed a week. He jes sleeps all time."

"Is he sick?"

"Not as I kin see. He jes old."

"How old?"

"Sugar, we got no way ov' tellin' de yars, but yo' Gran'ma say he is a hunert' an' five. An' she know cause he wuked fo' her gran'ma."

"Maybe he'll like some of this chicken soup my mother sent, and Aunt Deanna might, too. Here's some ham and pound cake, and Daddy sent a box of canned goods from the store; they want you to divide everything."

"I craves some ov' dat ham," said Mammy Lou.

"My teeth ain't so good no mo', so I look forward to de poun' cake wid buttermilk," said Uncle Reuben. "Whut de saddle fo'?"

"I'm going to ride Dan around. I've never seen where you buried my horse when he died."

Elizabeth and I helped Mammy Lou take in the food, and we divided it according to what they could use. When I came out, Uncle Reuben had unhitched and saddled Dan.

"Helping me just as you always did," I said, thanking him. "Please tell Elizabeth I'll be back with the drinks as soon as they're cool." Then, after speaking to Aunt Deanna, I was off, taking a shortcut to the back pasture, following Uncle Reuben's directions to the spot where he had buried my horse.

In the distance I could see the tree that marked the place, a leafy, spreading water oak in whose shade I had stopped many times during rides to cool off in warm weather. I found the grave to be as I knew Uncle Reuben would make it, free of grass and with a large rock for the headstone. I tied up Dan's reins and turned him loose to graze, then I sat under the tree, leaned my head against the lichened trunk, and closed my eyes. Of all the memories I held dear about Egypt, none were more so than those that clustered around my little horse. My thoughts went back to the day I got Clark and how we fattened him up.

My father had assigned Uncle Reuben, the kind old lotman who really knew horses, to help me with Clark.

We fed Clark according to Uncle Reuben's directions, and I curried him—oh, how I curried him, until all the dead hair came off and his true color came through—a dark red bay with a white star on his forehead. When he got so round and pretty, the cowhands wanted him back because, after all, he had been the best cow pony on the place, the swiftest and most surefooted. But they would never get their hands on him again. I sold a little orphan heifer that I raised on a bottle and with the proceeds, ordered from a catalog a youth saddle and bridle. Mamma made the pad to protect the sore spot. At last Clark was ready for us to put on a show, and everyone around gathered to see our first performance. When I went to Clark's right side to mount, my father got alarmed and said, "Wait! Horses are trained to be mounted from the left."

"Now, Boss," said Uncle Reuben reproachfully. "You knows de Baby can't do dat wid dat heavy brace. We don 'pared fo' her gittin' up on dat hoss."

"We could help her," suggested my father.

"Or use a stool," added my mother.

"Y'all means well," said Uncle Reuben, "but she wants to do dis by hers'ef. Dat hoss is awright."

I let the reins hang loose, a signal for Clark to stand still, and then nimbly mounted from the right side. My parents laughed. "We should never have doubted you, Uncle Reuben," apologized my mother, and my father agreed.

I let Clark walk, trot, and canter around the yard.

"You may ride him around the quarter pasture," said my father. This was the small pasture surrounding the house. "When you go out on the plantation, though, you must ride with me." That was fine for a while, but there was so much interesting work going on around the plantation and I was missing it.

One night at supper I brought up the subject. My parents stopped eating and gave me their attention.

"You think Clark and I do all right together, don't you?" They both agreed that we did. "Then don't you think it's time I rode out around the plantation?"

"Suppose you needed help with that heavy brace?" My father must have read my mother's mind. That was her worry also.

"I won't need it," I said, sure of myself.

"I have an idea," said my father, momentarily pushing back his plate of dewberry pie. "If you promise always to be within calling distance of some workmen or of a cabin that is occupied, then we might just try it. What do you think, Mamma?" She agreed, provided I would be sure to remember. I carried out their wishes, and before long an incident proved them to be right in their precautions.

I was sitting on Clark, allowing him to graze on a ditch bank while I watched some of the hands, the women hoeing and the men plowing, as they worked out the corn in Jolly

Bottom. The corn planted in this rich soil truly grew "as high as an elephant's eye." It had one enemy, the Johnsongrass. Although this grass made the finest hay, the gnarled roots could destroy any crop. I was watching with admiration the women's dexterity with their hoes, cutting out the grass without ever cutting a stalk of the young corn, when suddenly this peaceful scene was interrupted by Clark's jumping, rearing, and stomping his feet. Then I was stung on the leg and I realized that my horse had stepped in a yellow jackets' nest. One of the plowmen saw the situation and came running. He pulled me out of the saddle, slapped Clark to make him get out of the area, then ran with me to escape the angry insects that filled the air. We both got stung before making our getaway. This kind friend deposited me on the grass, and some of the women came running to help. They unbuckled my brace and pulled down my ribbed stocking.

"Chile, you got a heap o' stings on yo' leg. Som'n got to be done fo' you right now." The man who rescued me chewed a big wad of tobacco, and the women rubbed the bites with the juice. It was amazing how quickly the pain subsided and the swelling went down. I thought this occurrence was serious enough that I should relate it to my parents. They looked at my leg and were very concerned.

"You are all right now," both agreed, then my father said, "Tobacco juice is a very old remedy, and those people did the very best thing available. Also, they did it quickly, which is important." That night my parents walked back to the quarters to thank those people for their help.

As my parents allowed me to do, I rode to the cabins whose occupants were either too old or too young to go out to work, and I soon knew all their names. When weather permitted, the very elderly liked to sit on their cabin porches in the sun,

Shipping hay, when baled, was a big business on Egypt.

and as I sat nearby on my horse, they would tell me interesting stories, generally about Egypt. I especially enjoyed one about how the plantation got its name.

"Baby," one said, "you read de Bible story about how Joseph an' his brethren went down to de city ov' Egypt to buy de good grain dat dey was known fo'? Well, dis plantation hyar growed cawn jes as good in Jolly Bottom, so it wus come to be called Egypt jes lak dat city. Dis happened way back befo' de wah fo' freedom."

That night at supper I related the story to my parents and to Mr. Shedd, who was having the meal with us. They were most interested and upon inquiry found the story to be based on fact, as most were that were passed down by these old people.

The hay made for shipment was one of the two big money crops on Egypt. When summer and hay season were over, preparations were made for the other money business, which was the sale of beef cattle to northern markets. One of my fondest memories of riding Clark was my first participation in a cattle drive. Before my father allowed me to go, he prepared me by saying, "You know that Clark was trained to drive cattle. That means that without any directions from you, he will go after any cow that breaks away from the herd. He will do quick turns, and you have to be alert to stick on."

"I can do it," I had said.

"We'll see." He obviously was a little anxious, and he watched to see how well I did. He well might have been concerned because I had to employ all the tricks of staying on when Clark, with me in the saddle, chased his first stray cow. When my father was convinced I could manage, he ceased to worry although he frequently reminded me to be alert.

When my mother saw how brown and strong I was becoming by spending all my waking hours in the open, she was very happy and agreed with my doctors that this was a good way for me to regain my health after polio. But she did worry secretly that I would grow up to be a tomboy. I remembered how my father laughed at the idea when she finally expressed her fears. After I entered school, my mother's worries ended because even though all my life I would go horseback riding as often as I had the opportunity, my studies then claimed much of my time.

I was so engrossed in these childhood memories that I almost fell asleep, leaning against the tree trunk, when something startled me awake. It was Dan, nuzzling my neck. He was no doubt trying to tell me that it was time for his dinner. I put the reins over his neck and quickly climbed into the saddle. For a moment, I looked at Clark's grave.

"I'll never forget you," I whispered, then galloped back to join Elizabeth, stopping long enough at the watering trough to pick up the drinks.

Elizabeth was glad to see Dan and me and especially the cold drinks because the day had become very warm. We sat under the trees to eat. Our father had given us an assortment of soda pop, and Mammy Lou and Uncle Reuben drank some with us, as was intended. Mammy Lou gave Uncle Cajer a few sips as he lay in bed, and Aunt Deanna had one on her porch.

"Tell us some news," Mammy Lou begged. "We don't go nowhere no mo', an' we scacely sees foks."

"What would you like to know?" I asked.

"Well, fust, about y'awl. Is de baby growed much? Is yo' Pa gittin te lak de sto' bus'ness or do he miss us? An whut mischief Miss Lucy up to dese days?"

"Wait!" I laughed. "One thing at a time. Yes, little Wee has really grown. She's talking and into everything. Now about my father. I can tell you, he'll never forget you, and no he does not like store business. My mother works very hard because she misses all the help you all gave her, but I think she'll always have time for a little fun and mischief."

"An Mis 'Lizbeth, you sho' got pretty. Got you a beau yit?"

"A beau," I laughed. "About a dozen!"

"Aw, Tutter, you know better," she said.

"An' whut about you? You's good lookin'. Whar you' beaus dese days, Mis' Susie?"

"Every one of mine has gone away for one reason or another. I'm in a pure fix!"

"You'll catch one," said Uncle Reuben. "Don't worry 'bout dat." Uncle Reuben always believed in me.

Dan joined our picnic, eating the shelled corn Uncle Reuben prepared for him. Then Uncle Reuben brushed the old horse off while Elizabeth and I helped Mammy Lou clean up around the area.

When we were all finished, I climbed into the saddle again.

"Tutter, where are you going this time?" inquired Elizabeth.

"Through the big pasture, the prettiest part of Egypt."

"Miss Susie, I don't need ter 'mind you dat it ain't good to ride a hoss hawd on a full stomach," Uncle Reuben said.

"Not good for his stomach or mine?" I teased.

"Aw, go on. Yo' know I don't worry 'bout yo'," he said.

I went through the big gate and turned east. This used to be our prettiest hay field. Now I observed the quality of growth through which I was passing. One could see the base of Johnsongrass, but there was a mixture of weeds, black-eyed Susans, and a myriad of smaller blossoms, not now the best of hay. Suddenly Dan stopped and pricked up his ears. I was a little puzzled, then I remembered the covey of quail that ranged along here. When one came upon them, they could rise with such a whirr of wings as to make a horse jump from under a person.

Dan was a smart old horse. He walked cautiously, knowing the quail were there. When they saw us and rose with the noise I expected, I held the reins tightly and was able to stay safely in the saddle. I patted Dan on the neck.

"You are a good horse," I assured him.

Soon we came out of the field and crossed a pretty little branch, which was a tributary of the main creek. Now we were in the big pasture, and soon we came to the thicket that covered several acres.

It was a junglelike patch of trees and bushes that was purposely left in pastures to grow that way to provide cover for cattle in winter. Most of the large old plantations had them. I could still see the maze of small tunnel-like paths inside. I remembered the time I tried to walk into one of these paths.

I got so entangled with vines and briars that I was glad to get out. Thereafter, I agreed with my father that these thickets were for cows, not people.

Now Dan and I came to the most beautiful part of the big pasture. Its rolling meadows and little clumps of trees here and there were a typical picture of Alabama's Black Belt. I could remember when it was even prettier, with horses and cattle grazing on it. Soon we came to the main creek, so we followed its banks for nearly a mile under the shade of the cottonwood trees until we came to the crossing. There the banks were steep but sturdy and dried-up hoofprints showed that stock had crossed here in the past. The first time I crossed here on Clark, it was a little scary, but following my father's instructions to hold a tight rein going down and a loose one going up, while I held onto the horse's mane, I crossed safely. Now Dan and I did it with no trouble.

Soon I came to the other windmill and trough, and it was still working. I allowed Dan to rest and refresh himself while I climbed down and got a drink from the spout of the pump. Just then deep thunder sounded in the west.

Oh, dear, I thought. I knew that when it turned so unseasonably warm today, our pretty autumn weather would not last. Dan, we'd better get going. I climbed into the saddle and decided to go back by following the creek because not only was that shorter but it was the prettiest route. The foliage was not so dense on this side, affording a good view of the creek in all its beauty. In places it was almost like the tropics, with its glistening little pools, bordered by sandbars. In one pool, a large crane stood on one leg.

That bird is watching for crayfish, I thought. And I wished I could do a painting of the scene, catching not only the crane but its lifelike reflection in the water and the overhanging ferns.

I rode on, and then I saw something that made me rein in my horse. It was a large cottonmouth moccasin coiled under the overhanging opposite bank. Horses had been known to bolt at the sight of a snake, and I got Dan by in a hurry. Just then the thunder sounded deeper and much closer, and the sky in the west was turning a dark slate gray.

"Oh, my, I'd better go and pick up Elizabeth in a hurry." I took an even more direct route and put Dan into a brisk trot, anxious to get the buggy over the plantation road before the rain.

12

Minnie Runs Away

THE CHILDREN WERE SLOW TO TAKE PART IN THE games that I taught them but gradually found they were fun and began to look forward to what they called recess. I told them not to feel so bad about the weather because I had a book to read to them at playtime. Soon they became so engrossed in *Little Lord Fauntleroy* that they hated to see me put it down.

They all wanted to know where England was when I read that Cedric and his mother were going there. The children located England on the globe, then they found New York, where the book's characters had sailed from, and the Atlantic Ocean that they had crossed. I was glad to see them using the globe on their own.

Even though the rains did not let up, I continued driving from home, but travel got harder each day. Some low places were already so deep and boggy that I could make it through them only by putting on all the power the little car had. Afterward, the car looked as if it had had a mud bath.

I was sure that my time of living at home was short, and my
father had already arranged for me to stay with a family, a Mr.
and Mrs. Penney and their daughter, Miss Sarah, whom I had
met. So I would not have to dip into my salary to pay for room
and board, he offered the Penneys two fine Jersey heifers that
he had. They wanted the heifers for their dairy but felt he was
giving too much.

"I don't think so," he said, "and anyway we don't have room
where we are now for so much stock." I am sure he was thinking of the feed bill, too, because he had no place in Spring
Hill to raise hay and grain as he had on Egypt.

It seemed that the rains would never cease, but finally there
was a change in the weather, and one morning I awoke with
the sun in my eyes. I looked out and saw that it was a beautiful
day with the wet autumn leaves sparkling on the trees. The
weather had turned cooler, but I hoped the sun would be warm
enough to dry up the roads a little, thus enabling me to drive
from home a while longer.

That morning as I started toward the school, I noticed that
no farmers were in the fields today. Perhaps the ground was too
waterlogged, but mud or no mud, I thought, the children and
I would play outside that day. I always looked forward to seeing
the children on the porch, waiting for me, and they were always there, rain or shine, but when I came in view of the
school, strangely no one was in sight. Smoke was coming
out of the chimney, showing that Dan had built a fire. I could
not understand it. As I came closer, I realized that someone
was walking around in the yard. It was Reverend Milford, and
he had something on his shoulder. Was it—yes, it was—
a gun!

My mouth went dry as I drove into the yard. Reverend
Milford did not speak. This was the man who had scowled at

us in the door that first day when he had seen Minnie waving at the window.

I had an impulse to run into the schoolhouse and lock the door, but I would not permit myself to do that. Instead, I went over and laid my hand on Reverend Milford's arm.

"Is—is it Minnie?"

"She's done run off with that scoundrel, Cluster. I'll kill him."

"Please, Reverend Milford," was all I could say. Then I hurried in to the children. They were huddled together and, of course, Lily was in tears. I took her hand. There was nothing I could say to comfort them or to change the disturbed expressions on those usually serene faces.

"We don't know where Minnie is," said Cammie, beginning to cry. "She just wasn't in her bed this morning." Dimmie, usually so in control of her feelings, began to give way to the thought that their oldest sister was gone for good.

There was a soft knock at the back door, and Dan went to open it. It was Mrs. Milford.

"Miss Susie," she said, "I jes had to come to see you. We in such trouble." She wiped her eyes with her apron. "My husband sets such great store by that child."

"Mrs. Milford," I said, "I think you have to realize that Minnie just isn't a child anymore. I think she is very serious about that young man."

"Yes'm, I think so, too, but my husband, he jes can't take it." She lifted her apron and wiped her eyes again. "But he ain't a bad man, Miss Susie. He ain't never hurt nobody, and it would be jes awful if he shot that boy. He's fond of you, Miss Susie, even tho he don't show it. Won't you hep us? Jes talk to him, please, ma'am."

"Do you think he'd listen to me, Mrs. Milford?"

"I think he would. He's got a quick temper but he gits over

it. Now I got to go. He'd be mad, did he know I wus here."
Dan opened the back door, and the troubled woman went
back through the cotton field the way she had come.

I stood up and squared my shoulders. I did not know that
such things went with teaching. The children hung to me
begging, "Don't go—please don't go."

"Oh, he won't hurt me," I said, trying to assure myself as
well as the children. I went to the bookshelves that Dan and
his father had just built for me. "Here is a book of stories.
Debra, do you think you could read one to the children? And
Dan, maybe it would be good to bring in some more wood
for the fire. If you'd put it under the stove maybe it would
dry out."

Then I went out to Reverend Milford. I had never hated to
do anything so much in my life. I took him by the arm.

"Reverend Milford, come and sit on the steps with me. I
know you are upset about Minnie. We all are."

He looked down at me. In his eyes was not so much anger
now as sorrow. "You love her, too, don't you, Miss Susie?" He
had never talked to me so kindly.

"Yes, I do. She is a sweet girl, but maybe she is troubled
right now. I know you are, too. But Reverend Milford, I'm
afraid you still think of her as a little girl. And she just isn't
anymore. She is seriously in love, or at least she thinks she is."
I could not believe I was doing it, but I took the gun out of his
hand and laid it on the porch; then we sat down together on
the steps.

Reverend Milford wiped his eyes on his sleeve, then he said
to me, "Miss Susie, what am I going to do?" The words could
have come from Toby, he sounded so helpless.

"Reverend Milford, you know I have not had experience in
such things, but I think the first thing to do is to find Minnie

and Cluster. Then, if you could, peacefully talk things over with them. What are your greatest worries about Minnie?"

"Well, in the first place, Miss Susie, she ain't old enough— jes sixteen. She was sickly when she was little, an' I reckon her Maw an' me, we spoiled her—leastways, she don't know nuthin' 'bout what it takes to be a wife."

"And the boy, Cluster?"

"Tell you the truth, Miss Susie, we don't know a heap about 'im. Could be, he ain't all that bad. But we don't know kin he tak keer of Minnie or not. He slips aroun' to see her."

"Do you know where he lives"?

"No, not 'zactly—somer's—south o' here, I reckon. Leastways, Minnie met him at camp meetin'."

"Reverend Milford, do you know the ministers down in that area?"

"Yes'm. I've preached down there."

"Well, you know Minnie and Cluster might not know that your intentions are good. Maybe you could find a minister who knows Cluster and his family and he could sort of be a go-between—or whatever you call it. But Reverend Milford, don't you think, for Minnie's sake, you and Cluster are going to have to get to know each other?"

"Yes'm—I reckon so. If only he had come right out an' ast me in the first place."

"Do you think you were ready to listen?"

"No'm—I reckon not. I felt like I wanted to kill 'im. But Miss Susie, I don't really want to hurt nobody. I had enough of feudin' an killin' when I wust growin' up—in the mountains 'way up north o' here. When Minnie wuz born, my wife an' me we decided to move down here. We didn't want to bring up no family thataway."

"I'm glad you told me," I said, getting up. For the first time I felt that maybe I understood his violence. "But may I say one more thing. If you get Minnie back—and I hope you do—I think you are going to have to let them see each other. You know, in some way that you approve. Then maybe they won't be slipping around. You don't think they could already be married, do you?"

"I'm afeared of it."

"Well, she is not of age, so it might take time. If she comes back, I'll do all I can to make her happy at school."

"You've a-ready done that. I owe you a lot, Miss Susie." He picked up the gun. Again I took it out of his hand.

"Reverend Milford, I don't believe it would be safe for you to walk down the road now with a gun. You know how gossip gets around in a little place. Suppose Cluster or some of his family saw you with a gun. They might shoot you first and ask questions later. Let's hide it someplace. Then the children and I will bring it to you after school."

"Well'm, I'd sho' hate to lose it. I do some huntin' to get meat fo' the table. Preachin' don't bring in much."

"Please unload it, Reverend Milford. I'm scared of loaded guns."

He did so; then we walked around back and hid the gun under piles of kindling.

"Thank you, Miss Susie," he said. "Now I got a lotta prayin' to do, an' I won't waste no time tryin' to contact that preacher to hep me find Minnie."

"The very best of luck," I said. I watched him go and stood there lost in thought. I was certainly seeing a side of life I had never known. I wondered if I could have learned as much in a year at college. Maybe not, in some ways.

Dan stuck his head out of the door. "He gone Miss Susie?"

"Yes," I said, bringing my thoughts back to the problems at

hand. I went in to the children. Debra was just finishing a story. They were anxious to hear about what had happened.

"I don't think Reverend Milford is angry anymore—just worried—and wants to find Minnie. He has a plan so maybe he will find her."

Minnie's little sisters were inconsolable. I had a plan for Thanksgiving which I had meant to discuss with them after lessons were over. Maybe, I thought, it might help matters to do it now.

"Have any of you thought about Thanksgiving? It is only three weeks away." There was no response. They did not seem to care one way or another. I continued.

"We get out on the Wednesday before. How would you like to give a little party that day and invite your parents and any other family that you have?" The word *party* aroused their interest.

"W-W-What would we do?" asked Dan.

"First," I said, "we could put some of our best work up for your parents to see. Then after that, we'd serve refreshments. Debra, do you think you could bake one of your chocolate cakes? Tell your mother it is for Thanksgiving, but we'd want the party to be a surprise. Then I'd make a big bowl of punch. The rest of you could help me with that."

"I'd love to bake the cake," said Debra.

"My Ma is teaching me to bake pound cakes," said Ellie. "Would you like me to try one, Miss Susie?"

"That would be wonderful. Dan, that chinquapin tree was so loaded. Would you have time to get some more? We still have a few left from last time." Dan thought he could.

"When all are seated, we could open with a Scripture reading. You remember, I read to you the Twenty-Third Psalm. Don't you think that in three weeks we could memorize it? And we'd open the program with that."

"I know we could," said Cammie. "I almost know it already."

"What else could we do?" asked Dimmie.

"I know how to make a hand-turn movie out of a box, two broom handles, and a long strip of wrapping paper. I could draw pictures of the Thanksgiving story, and all of you could help color them. I'll write the story and Debra, you could tell it as the boys turn the movie. I'll find something for everyone to do. You know we've been learning the pledge of allegiance to the flag so we could say that."

"I think the parents would like that," said Debra. "Our sister who is a nurse may be here. Could I invite her?"

"Please do," I said. I noticed that Dan seemed to be feeling a little uncomfortable. I thought I understood.

"Dan," I said, "I want you to be the master of ceremonies."

"W-W-What's that?"

"Well, I'd like you to meet people at the door and show them where to sit. Toby, maybe you could help Dan. Then Dan, I'd like you to help us in any way possible."

"And Dimmie, you could call out names of people on the program." She smiled at that, and Dan seemed relieved that he was not going to have to recite a poem or tell a story. Toby seemed a little hurt. He thought he had been left out.

"You, Toby, are going to be very important. You are going to end our program by saying a poem called 'Chistopher Robin Is Saying His Prayers.' That is, if you'd like to do it. I'll bring a copy tomorrow. Now we'd better get busy with lessons."

I was relieved to see the usual happy atmosphere restored. Even the little mouse was there, waiting for its crumbs. I only wished that I could feel happier. I looked around at all the colorful paintings Minnie had done to brighten up our room. Suppose she never came back. Would the little school ever be the same without her?

13

The Thanksgiving Party

ON FRIDAY NIGHT AFTER SUPPER, I EXCUSED MYSELF from the family and went out to sit in the porch swing where I could be alone to reflect on events of the past week. It was really too chilly to sit out so I wrapped my mother's shawl about me.

There was also Christmas to think about. It was hardly a month away. I wondered what small gifts I could afford for the schoolchildren, and I worried about my own family. My parents had always made Christmas a big and beautiful affair in our home, but now I felt sure that my father was no more than getting by in his store. Even customers of long standing were trading more and more in Demopolis because there was a wider selection there and that road had been graveled. So far, I had not broken my vow to save every penny of my small salary for college, and I hoped I could stick to it, but surely there must be some way to earn a few extra dollars for Christmas.

I was so deep in thought that I was not aware that a vehicle had stopped at the front gate. It was about dark, and it was only when the rusty gate hinges creaked that I realized someone was coming into the yard.

"Miss Susie," called a voice, barely above a whisper. "That you, Miss Susie?"

"Minnie," I cried, hurrying down the steps and up the path. "Oh Minnie! We've been so worried about you."

"I'm sorry. I didn't mean to worry nobody, especially you. I forgot—this Cluster, Miss Susie."

"Cluster, I'm so glad to meet you."

He came forward and timidly shook my hand. "I feel like I know you, Miss Susie. Minnie talks about you so much. We hated to bother you, but Minnie wouldn't talk to nobody else."

"I'm glad you came. Both of you come in the house."

"No'm," said Minnie. "We jes want to talk to you private like. Won't you sit with us? It's warm in the front seat of the truck." When we were seated, Minnie continued. "See, Miss Susie, we got word from Pa. Seems like he wants to talk to us, peaceable like. We jes' wondered, did he mean it—he said anything to you, Miss Susie?"

"Yes, he did." (I did not intend to mention the gun.) "But tell me, first, are you married?"

"No. You see, Miss Susie," said Cluster, "it would take time to get a license here, Minnie being so young an' all. Anyways, we'd like to wait awhile. Minnie's been stayin' with my folks, but I want better'n that for her. See, for 'bout a year I been buying this piece of land—it's good land—we kin raise things on it. An' it's got a house. The house needs a lot done to it. I been fixin' it up on my off time and it'll take a while. I want things nice for Minnie."

"Miss Susie," said Minnie, "it's got big trees in the front yard, all red and gold now. The kind you like."

"I'd surely like to see it. You asked about your father—yes, he did talk to me and he seems ready to let you all see each other if you'll come home. And we surely miss you at school. We are getting ready for a Thanksgiving party, but it won't be the same without you."

"I'd like to finish out this year of school," she said, "but Miss Susie, if Pa don't let me see Cluster, I ain't never comin' home."

"I think things will work out for you," I said, "but it seems to me that the only way is for both of you to go right away and talk things over with your father."

"Yes'm, I reckon you're right."

"And there is another thing we have to decide. The county fair opens on Monday. If you want to enter your painting, it should be there by then."

"I go right by there every day," said Cluster. "I could take it for you."

"Well," said Minnie with a sigh, "effen we works things out with Pa."

They thanked me and rode away.

On Monday morning Minnie was back at school. Whatever had transpired between her, Cluster, and her father must have been pleasant because she hummed happily as she worked at a painting. I paused by Minnie's paint table to admire her work. It was of a house with big trees around it.

"Is that the place Cluster is buying?" I asked.

"Yes'm—and guess what, Miss Susie? Pa is going to help him fix the house up. He said so."

"He is!" Things were going better than I had ever hoped they would. Cluster passed at the usual times in his logging truck, but now Minnie might glance toward the windows and smile but there was no tension as before.

During the weekend, Mr. Douglas, with some help from Mr. Tucker, had finished repairing the well. They had had the water tested, and it was found to be safe. These thoughtful men had even added a chain, two buckets, and a pulley so that now drawing up a bucket of water could be fun. All of us took turns trying it. Even though the weather was cooler, it was still refreshing to have a drink every so often from a dripping bucket whose contents came from deep in the cool well. Only people who had no electricity and consequently no cooling devices could fully appreciate this luxury. The water came in especially handy when we were washing pitchers and jelly glasses to make them sparkle for the party.

There were more little details to planning a party than I had realized. No one around had a punch bowl so we settled for a few pretty pitchers. If paper cups were made in those days, I did not know it; therefore, the neighbors donated jelly glasses and the church loaned me some small decorative plates. The punch would actually be lemonade, but my mother said she would put in red cake coloring to make it pretty and some of her canned fruit. Ice had to be brought more than ten miles and then had to be kept packed in sawdust until the time it was needed. Mr. Douglas said he would take care of that.

All knew their parts, and Toby gave a fine rendition of A. A. Milne's Christopher Robin saying his prayers, but one problem arose. Toby declared that he would never come out in front of people wearing pajamas.

"Then how about in a man's robe?" I suggested. (I knew it would never do to call it a dressing gown.) Toby thought about it a while and decided that a man's robe would be all right, and he was also willing to wear bedroom slippers and carry a lighted candle. His mother was very interested and went about getting his costume ready. Cammie, Ellie, and Lily would stand to the side of the stage and recite the opening and closing stanzas.

Minnie was to show her pretty framed painting, and now she was making drawings of the Thanksgiving story to show while Debra told it. My father had donated the wrapping paper and the broom handles and also a large box for the handmade movie, which Dan and Toby would operate. I had brought pictures of the Pilgrims and Indians to help Minnie get her illustrations just right for the story.

Miss Bunker had not been to the school lately, which I felt sure was because of the bad roads. The children had made an invitation to the party for her, which I had mailed, and I was a little glad Miss Bunker had not been there because all they were doing would now be a surprise.

I wished my own family could come, but there was no way because I was using the family car. My mother still had her horse and buggy, but the distance was too great for that.

The afternoon before the party, the fathers of the children, with Dan's help, arranged the seating. They made a semicircle of desks at the back, with benches in front of them. Dan's mother said she would bring some of her patchwork quilts in case children needed to sit on the floor.

The day of the party was a typical gray November day, very cold, with a misty rain, which in the afternoon turned to fine sleet. But inside, the little school was warm and cozy and as pretty as the children and I could make it. They had worked hard, they knew their parts well, and they thought how awful it would be if the weather kept people from coming. They watched the sky anxiously.

The party had been set for three o'clock, but now I wished I had made it earlier. I need not have worried. All the families, anxious about the weather, came early. First was Miss Sarah Penney, whom I had invited. I had asked her to help Cammie and Ellie at the refreshment table. She had brought not only two pies but one of her prettiest tablecloths. By putting Minnie's paint table and my desk together, we had room for everything. In the center were Debra's and Ellie's cakes and Miss Sarah's lemon meringue pies and at the back, the pitchers of colorful punch. Dan had contributed a bowl of chinquapins and little sprigs of holly full of red berries from a tree he had found.

I was proud of the children, who had worn their Sunday best, and especially of my two boys, who graciously met people at the door and seated them.

Miss Bunker arrived early. She had a young man, Eddie, she called him, driving for her because she had not yet gotten accustomed to the winter roads.

"I want you to know," she said to me, "I put off my visit home for a day in order to get to this party." She brought little dishes of nuts and mints which gave a finished look to the table. I thought Lily needed more responsibility so I told her that she might pass the nuts and mints after people were served.

Toby whispered to Dan that he wanted to escort Miss Bunker to a seat. Ever since she had helped him with reading, she was a very special lady to him. He stood by her, as tall and straight as he could, and held out his arm. She took it, although she towered far above him, and he escorted her to the best seat in the house, where she would have a good view of the stage.

The Douglases came with the ice and a tub for washing off the sawdust.

"Miss Susie," said Mr. Douglas with a laugh, "we don't

really need no ice today. We could set the punch here on the porch, an it 'ud freeze by itse'f."

"Yes," I answered, "but after all your trouble, let's use it. It will make the punch sparkle."

"We'd better wait until we're ready to use it," suggested Mrs. Douglas.

"I guess so," I said, "but don't you miss the part that Toby will do."

"We wouldn't," they declared.

When all the families had arrived and were seated, Dimmie came out to welcome them. She and I had discussed what would be nice to say to the parents and friends, and I encouraged her to put it in her own words. She did so, and it sounded very natural and appropriate. Then I got up and told them that I thought Dimmie had expressed quite well how happy we all were to have them. I wanted to add only that I thought they could be proud of how hard their children had worked to make it a good party.

Next, I introduced Miss Bunker and told them how much she had meant to our school. Miss Bunker stood up.

"Friends," she said, "I can't tell you how glad I am to be a part of this little school. They have done so much with so little, and it's such a happy little school. I am not exaggerating when I say that I am more proud of it than of any school in the county." She sat down, and there was much applause. The audience was certainly with us, and I think they wanted to express their appreciation by applauding everything we said and did.

"Now," I said, "the children have learned a very beautiful Scripture which they will open with, followed by the pledge of allegiance to the flag." The children stood in a row, and Dimmie said, "Please bow your heads." I had told them I would be just behind the curtain in case they needed me, but they did it without a bobble.

After reciting the Twenty-Third Psalm, they faced the opposite wall, where the flag hung, and with their hands over their hearts, they gave the pledge of allegiance. I was bursting with pride over them, and I could tell that the parents were very impressed. The children went to the back, and I came out again.

"I'm sure you know that reading is one of our most important subjects. Two of our youngest have each chosen a page to read for you. Dimmie will announce them."

First, she called Toby, now in a hard primer, and then Lily, in an advanced third reader. I couldn't refrain from peeping out to watch Miss Bunker's face. It was filled with pleased surprise. She told me later that she could not believe they had advanced so far.

Toby and Lily got much applause. Then Dimmie, Cammie, Ellie, and Lily sang the Thanksgiving song, beginning "Over the river and through the woods."

After that I came out with Minnie. Minnie was holding her framed painting, which now had a blue ribbon on it.

"Friends," I said, "I'm sure you will be glad to hear about an honor which Minnie Milford has won. Her painting was given first prize, five dollars, at the county fair." Again there was applause and many "ah's" and "oh's."

"Now," I said, "I want to introduce a student who is a wonderful storyteller, Debra Tucker. As she tells us the story of the first Thanksgiving, Dan and Toby will show you a movie of it with illustrations by Minnie Milford and colored by all of the children." Debra did so well that I was glad that her older sister, the nurse, was there to hear her.

After the story, we went behind a little screen for the finale,

Toby's Christopher Robin. We put a sheet over a low table to serve as his bed, and we had covered the back windows so Toby and his lighted candle would stand out. I hoped no one told him how adorable he looked as he came out and kneeled by the "bed" because I knew he would not like that. Then Ellie, Cammie, and Lily gave the introductory stanza.

"Little boy kneels at the foot of his bed, drops on his little hands, little gold head. Hush! Hush! Whisper who dares! Christopher Robin is saying his prayers."

Then Toby gave a fine impersonation of a small boy saying his prayers and forgetting now and then and talking about other things. When he got to the end and said, "Now what was the other I had to say? I said 'bless Daddy' so what can it be?"

I had told him to pause here, but he did it so long that his mother was in a panic that he had forgotten his lines. Then he practically shouted, "Now I remember it—God bless me!"

The applause was so great that the girls' last stanza was drowned out, but the party was a success and I think everyone present was proud of our eight children. They had learned to speak before an audience, but I felt that maybe Dan had passed the greatest milestone because even though his part was small, his was the most difficult for him to do. Now Miss Sarah took over the program.

"Friends," she said, "even though I have no children in this school, I am as proud of it as if I had. I have heard such interesting things about what they do here. Not only do they work at the three R's, but they paint, they go on nature walks, their teacher walks a log and falls in the creek, and they have so much love here that they have adopted as a pet, a little mouse." When the laughter subsided, I pointed to the far end of a rafter and there it sat. Some laughed but a few of the ladies shuddered.

"Don't worry," I said. "It is not accustomed to so much noise, and I doubt if it will come any closer—especially if Dan will give it some cake crumbs."

"But seriously," continued Miss Sarah, "I think this is more than a party. It is the first time our community has gotten together in a long time. Somehow we have become a part of this school and the school a vital part of our community." The people all stood and clapped and Reverend Milford said, "Amen."

I tried to say thank you but was too touched to make the words come out.

"Now," said Miss Sarah, "after Reverend Milford gives us a blessing, let's all eat and drink and be merry."

14

Home for the Holidays

THE WARMTH AND HAPPINESS OF THAT THANKSGIVING party seemed to be felt by all, and it was something I always remembered. The parents seemed especially appreciative of the chance to see their children perform, and I remembered that too.

As the weather became worse, I could sense a feeling of uneasiness among them. Except for the Milfords, they were all farmers, and I could understand their need to hurry home to do the milking and other chores.

"Miss Susie," said Dan, "I rally need to go home and help my Pa, but I'll come back one day to sweep, bring in wood, and do anything else that needs doing."

He had finally accepted the five dollars a month that the superintendent had suggested and was taking the job very seriously, doing more than was required.

The men quickly helped him arrange the desks and benches back in place and take down the make-do curtains. Some of the children were reluctant to leave, feeling they might be needed, but I waved them off, saying, "Have a nice Thanks-giving and I'll see you Monday morning." Soon only Miss Sarah, Miss Bunker, her driver, Eddie, and I were left.

"Miss Sarah," I said, "I want to take a minute to talk with you. I think the time has come for me to board with you and your parents, if that is all right."

"Of course. I think you should."

"One thing worries me," I continued. "I can't keep the family car because they will need it. I have been wonder-ing how—"

"Say no more. You are wondering how you'll get to school each day. Well, Mr. Douglas and I have already discussed it and between us we'll get you there. When will you come back?"

"I'll get back sometime Sunday even if I have to ride a horse to do it."

"No need for that. You can get to Linden, can't you? I'll meet you there. I've learned to cope with that road in winter."

"Maybe I can help out," interrupted Miss Bunker. "I'll be coming back from visiting my folks on Sunday and it would be very little out of my way to go by Spring Hill and pick you up, Susie, say, about three o'clock? The Linden train station would be a convenient place for you two to meet and it would be warm, so, Susie, I'll let you out there."

"Well 'warm' is something to think of today," said Miss Sarah, gathering up her belongings. "Listen to that wind." It was howling around the little building, and sleet was hitting the windows, sounding like small pellets on glass. "Susie, I'm worried about your getting home over those roads."

"Would it be too much out of your way to go by Linden with us?" asked Miss Bunker. "From there on, you'd have a graveled road, you know."

"It would be about twice as far, but I've been consider-ing it."

"Then it's all settled. Let's get going."

"Miss Sarah, would you please call my father at the store and tell him I'll be late. I'd hate for him to come out in this weather looking for me."

"I'll hurry home and do it. Good-bye."

I locked the door, and the two of us pulled our scarves and coats about us to face the wind and sleet.

Eddie held the car door open for Miss Bunker, but she sud-denly waved it shut, turned, and ran to my car.

"Open up, Susie. I'm going to ride with you. I have some-thing to tell you. Let's get over this bad stretch of road first."

I followed Eddie, attempting to stay in his tracks because he seemed to know what he was doing. At one especially boggy place, he left the road entirely and went through the pasture where the owner had obligingly let the fence down for that purpose.

I was anxious to hear what Miss Bunker had to tell me, but I waited patiently. When we were over the worst places, Miss Bunker turned to me.

"You told me that you'd like to earn some Christmas money, didn't you?"

"Oh, yes. Do you have an idea?"

"Yes, I do. You told me you made spending money in college by painting family coats-of-arms for faculty members, did you not?"

"Yes, Ma'am."

"Well, I brought one with me which I'll show you when we stop. It's of my mother's family and belongs to my brother. I borrowed it for you to see. If you could copy it, I could give you an order for three. Are you interested?"

"I surely am, if I can do it to suit. Could I keep it through the holidays?"

"Yes. I borrowed it for that long in case you wanted to try it. Would twenty-five dollars apiece be enough?"

"Too much. I didn't charge my teachers that much."

"No—it's worth that, at least. We would not pay any less because there is much detail. That would let you earn seventy-five dollars. Would that be enough to get you by?"

"Oh, Miss Bunker, that would be a dream come true."

"You'd be helping me, too. My mother has long wanted a coat-of-arms of our family. My sister wants one, and so do I. Those would help solve my problem of finding suitable Christmas presents. Now here we are at your road. Pull over to the side and have a look at what I have here."

It was a pretty coat-of-arms. I had done a good many similar ones.

"Well, Susie, what do you think?"

"I think I can do it. I'd like to try."

"I'll see you Sunday and we'll discuss this further. Have a happy Thanksgiving."

"You too." And we went our separate ways.

I had no problem with the roads the rest of the way for even though those old graveled roads were far from good, I could generally avoid the holes and slush, and certainly they were never slick or boggy. My going was slow because the sleet had become heavier and began caking the windshield with ice, making visibility poor. Twice I had to get out to scrape the ice off.

Twilight was coming earlier now. I turned on the lights, not that they helped me very much, but at least I could be seen by other travelers who were very, very few today. When at last I pulled into my yard, it was with a sigh of relief.

Mine were not the only sighs of relief. Even though Miss Sarah had called, explaining why I would be late, my family was very anxious about my being out in such weather. They practically pulled me in the door, and while brushing off the sleet they peppered me with questions. "Are you all right? Did you have any trouble? Are you warm?"

There was a roaring fire of logs in the living room. I flung off my heavy wraps and sank into an easy chair.

"I am just fine," I said, "and things couldn't be better."

Then, becoming aware of the odor of roasting turkey, I jumped up and followed my nose to the kitchen, with the family not far behind. There on the side table, cooling, were not only the delicious-looking turkey and dressing but mince pies and a big coconut cake.

"Oh my," I exclaimed, "Mamma, you and Rosa have done it again."

"Yes'm, us sho did," sighed Rosa. "An de wustest thing, wus pickin' dat tu'key. You know Mammy Lou always done dat at Egypt so's she could have de tu'key tail fo' a fan to take to chetch."

Rosa's words brought me a wave of homesickness for Egypt with the many loving black hands, anxious to help, and at night the singing in the quarters. I quickly changed the subject.

"I'm starving to death." I stuck my finger into the dressing and put it in my mouth.

"Stop that!" said my mother, playfully spanking me on the rear. Then she took a kitchen spoon and filled it with a large portion of the dressing. "Now, don't any of you do any more tasting. That goes for you, too, Daddy. I see you eyeing that coconut cake."

This remark about my father and the coconut cake brought

back memories of childhood Christmases. The family custom of leaving a slice of cake and a glass of milk by the chimney on Christmas Eve for Santa was our father's idea, and it always meant that my mother had to cut her best coconut cake before Christmas Day. It was also my father's idea that Santa's favorite cake was coconut. I winked at him.

"Daddy," I said, "you might as well accept the fact that you are not going to get a slice of that cake tonight."

"That's our Thanksgiving dinner," said my mother happily. "Aunt Frances and her family are coming tomorrow to bring grandmother, who is going to stay a while."

"Oh, wonderful, but can they come in this weather?" I asked.

"I think it may clear off," said my father. As a farmer he had always needed to watch the weather, and his predictions were usually right.

"I'm so hungry now," I said licking the last bit of dressing from the spoon. "What is there that we can eat now?"

"Vegetables left over from dinner, and in the oven are hot, roasted sweet potatoes and corn bread."

I hurried to help set the dining table. Remembering that I had been too excited to eat anything all day, I wanted to hurry things up, but Rosa and Elizabeth were ahead of me and the table was ready. "You can get the milk from the dairy," they said.

There was a long safe on the back porch where we kept all the products from our fine Jersey cow—long pans of milk, nearly an inch deep in cream, clabber where the milk had turned and cream had been skimmed off for churning, cakes of butter, and both kinds of milk. We called this safe the dairy. I filled two pitchers, one with sweet and the other with buttermilk, and took them to the table, where the others were already laying platters of food.

"Come on, Wee," I said, catching up my baby sister. "Let's get our hands washed." Since we did not have indoor plumbing, each bedroom held old-fashioned washstands with bowls and pitchers, the latter filled with water. Slop jars held the used water. When we had dried our hands, I reached for a brush.

"No, no," cried Wee, pulling away. She hated having her hair combed and brushed.

"Wait," I said. "I know how it hurts to get tangles out because I had curls like you when I was a little girl."

"You did?"

"Yes, and you see I'm not going to comb it, just brush it a little. You want to look pretty, don't you?"

"Yeah." But I could not detain her long. Our father was waiting for us before he asked the blessing. After that, I told them all about the party.

"When are we going to decorate the Christmas tree?" asked Elizabeth.

"The week before Christmas, as always. Oh, that reminds me—I want to borrow our ornaments for the tree at school because we don't have any."

"Then what will we do?"

"Elizabeth, you worry too much. Our school is out December 16 and I promise to bring them all back, safe and sound."

After supper was over and dishes washed, I called Elizabeth aside.

"I want you to help me with something. Can you keep a secret?"

Elizabeth was a little suspicious about my secrets, especially after I had given her a haircut such as I said they wore at

Montevallo, with the result that Elizabeth had to wear a hat to school for two weeks, but she was curious.

"What's the secret?"

"You see, this is going to be about the hardest Christmas Mamma and Daddy ever had, and it's up to you and me to make it a good one."

"How will we do that? I don't have a cent."

"We'll go to Demopolis on Friday, just you and me. First, I'll go to Robinson Banking Company and cash a check from my school money."

"Oh Tutter, you can't do that!"

"But you see, Elizabeth, I've got this Christmas job of painting a family coat-of-arms, and I can put it all back."

"Wel-l'l, if you are sure to do that. For how much?"

"Seventy-five dollars, that is, if I can do the painting. I'm sure I can. We'll go to Mayer Brothers and to other stores, too. We'll buy pretty but useful things like sweaters and material for Mamma to make skirts and dresses and things like that." Elizabeth was looking at her feet.

"What's the matter?"

"I need some dress shoes. I don't have any to wear to the Christmas parties."

"We'll buy those first," I said. Elizabeth was so pretty, with golden brown curls and expressive brown eyes, that it tugged at my heart to see her doing without, something we had never had to do before. We did not realize that the Great Depression was just ahead, and doing without would be the order of the day for most people. Times were hard enough at the moment, but somehow our family seemed to be able to take the bad with the good.

In the night the sleet turned to rain, and by midmorning

the sun came out, as if the heavens were smiling down for Thanksgiving. The relatives came, and it was a happy day. After they left, all except my grandmother, who stayed for a visit, I settled down and tried my hand at painting the coat-of-arms. Then I showed both to my family.

"Yours is just as pretty," they said.

"I don't deserve much credit. I just copied it, but if you like it, maybe Miss Bunker will too."

On Friday, Elizabeth and I went to Demopolis to carry out our plans. The teller at the bank, who had known me since my childhood, was a little disturbed at my cashing a check for seventy-five dollars.

"But I thought this was for your returning to Montevallo," he said.

"Don't worry. I have a Christmas job. I can put it back, and I will."

We did all the shopping and were pleased with a snowsuit that we found for Wee. Last we went to the five and dime store to buy paper, ribbons, and cards for wrapping. We still had fifteen dollars left so I gave six to Elizabeth.

"What for, Tutter?" she asked.

"You said you didn't have any money, and I thought you'd like to buy a little gift for your homeroom teacher and something for your boyfriend." Her face lit up.

"Oh, thank you, Tutter. I would! Will you help me?"

We went in the drugstore next door.

"My friend is getting a camera for Christmas," she said. "I know he'd like an album, and they have pretty ones here for four dollars." With the two dollars left, she bought a box of chocolates for her teacher. "What about Grandmother?" Elizabeth asked.

"Mamma is having a shawl made, and part of the money I

have left will go for the yarn. And then we must get oysters on Christmas for Daddy."

At home, we locked ourselves in our rooms until all the packages were wrapped and ready to be hidden on a high closet shelf. We kept the material out because Mamma always made clothes for Christmas and we felt she would want that now. Rosa came in just as we were storing the last package. She immediately guessed our secret.

"My name on one?" she asked.

"Oh, goodness!" I exclaimed. "We forgot Rosa!"

"I knows better," replied Rosa. She had never yet been forgotten.

15

The Christmas Party

I WORKED MOST OF SATURDAY, PAINTING THE OTHER TWO coats-of-arms, and by three o'clock Sunday, when I was expecting Miss Bunker, all were finished and on the mantle for her inspection. She arrived almost on the dot, and after chatting with the family and meeting my grandmother, she viewed the coats-of-arms from all angles.

"To tell you the truth, Susie, I can hardly tell which is the original. I like yours best, though, because they are hand painted."

"Are you just trying to make me feel good, Miss Bunker?"

"You know me better than that. How did you get them so perfect?"

"To be honest, Miss Bunker, I traced them, then I just had to put on finishing touches and get the colors right. So I can't claim any credit for originality."

"In this case, getting them right was the main thing. I wouldn't be surprised if you didn't get some more orders from my family." She then wrote the check for seventy-five dollars, which I left with Elizabeth to deposit in the bank to replace my withdrawal.

"Miss Bunker, how about a slice of cake and a cup of coffee while Daddy is putting Susie's suitcases in the car?" suggested my mother.

"A cup of coffee would hit the spot, but I'd better forgo the cake. I'm trying to shed a few of these pounds," she laughed.

On the way to Linden, I told Miss Bunker about the fun Elizabeth and I had spending the seventy-five dollars.

"You really made Christmas for us, you know."

"Well, I'm glad. You surely made seventy-five dollars go a long way."

We found Miss Sarah waiting at the depot so Miss Bunker and I said good-bye and went our separate ways.

Back at school on Monday morning, the children and I had a happy reunion, but somehow, there was a little letdown feeling among us. Perhaps it was to be expected after all the excitement of last week's party.

"Our school year is about half over now," I reminded them, "and we must work hard at our lessons. But the weather is too cool to play out much so wouldn't you like to do something also for Christmas?"

Debra spoke. "I've been thinking about it. I'm goin' to bake a cake, but you know, Miss Susie, we don't have any money."

"I understand. I'm in the same fix, but I like presents best that people make—not buy." They all looked puzzled.

"Dan, can you still find the pretty holly with so many berries? You remember, you brought some for the party?"

"Y-Yes'm, there's plenty at a place deep in the w-woods not far from our house."

"Well, I thought that would make really unusual Christmas wreaths."

"What do ya do with 'em?" asked Toby.

"Why, you hang them on your doors or over your mantle to decorate for Christmas."

I took chalk and drew one on the blackboard, then I picked up a sack I had brought.

"See, I bought red crepe paper to make a big bow for each of you and this ball of green cord for tying on the holly. In the back of the car is some hay-bailing wire and cutters to make the frames. We have three weeks before holidays and in that time we can do a great deal. Boys, will you get the wire and cutters?"

Now enthusiasm was restored.

"We are going home to lunch today," said Debra, "and we'll bring back some holly so we can start on the wreaths."

We made one frame out of the wire, and then we got down to lessons until lunchtime. When we opened our lunch boxes, the odor of food brought the mouse; I was relieved that it was still there. Dan and Debra were leaving so I called to Dan.

"Did you take care of it while we were gone, Dan?"

"Yes'm, I came twice and gave it crumbs and water." I knew how busy Dan was with farm work, and I thought his compassion for a little animal confirmed what I had come to believe about his sweet nature.

Debra and Dan hurried home to lunch, and they returned with two big sacks of holly.

"We-we'll b-bring more tomorrow," said Dan.

We had enough time left on our lunch hour to make one wreath. They clasped their hands and gave audible exclamations to express their awe at its beauty. We had hooks on the wall in back of the room for our coats. I took my coat down and hung the wreath there.

"How many we gonna make?" asked Cammie with her usual giggle.

"Well, let's count. Don't you children want one for your parents? That's three. One for Miss Bunker and one for Miss Sarah, and I hope you'll make one for me! That's six, and maybe we could do an extra one in case we need it."

"There's a box in the car," said Toby. "Somen's in it."

"Oh yes! I forgot. I brought our Christmas tree ornaments to decorate a tree. Maybe tomorrow we can go to the woods to look for one."

Next day at lunch hour, we went for the walk. The children chose a cedar, just the right size and thick with branches. We put it in a bucket of sand to keep it fresh and then for the next three weeks, in addition to lessons, we worked hard on decorating it and making wreaths. Minnie had the idea of drawing little Santas, clowns, balls, and animals, which they cut out and painted, and this added a touch of originality.

"Children, you know that big sweet gum tree by the road?" They nodded. "I notice that the ground is covered with last year's balls. If painted they make good decorations." Several of the children went out and came back with a sack full, which they painted in all colors.

I showed them how they could add little twigs of pine needles to the holly for variety, and the wreaths got prettier as we thought of new ideas. When they got ready to make my wreath, they retired to the back of the room and said I must not look. When finished, they hung it but covered it with paper to keep it as a surprise. While they were doing this, I looked through the stacks of books I had brought and found *The Night Before Christmas*. When they came back to the group, I asked them to sit around my desk. I held the book up.

"How many of you have ever read or heard this poem?" Only a few had.

"A long time ago a man by the name of Clement Moore wrote this. I'm sure he never thought it would be so popular. As long as you live, you will hear this read in one place or another on Christmas."

"Read it, please, ma'am," they all begged. So I gave it my best rendition. I think they loved it, as I always had.

"But there ain't no Santa Claus," said Toby in a tone of disappointment.

"Well," I said, "if you think of Santa as the spirit of giving, as something just in your mind, it makes a beautiful story. That way there really is a Santa Claus. I thought that if we read this every day, maybe by Christmas we could say it."

"For another p-p-program?" stammered Dan. He had improved in his shyness but was still insecure about talking in public.

"Not necessarily. Mainly, just for your own enjoyment."

"I want to try," said my little Lily, and they all agreed. After that, we read it daily—sometimes while we were eating lunch. One day Toby announced that he could say the reindeers' names, and he said them perfectly.

Some weeks earlier, Miss Sarah had obliged me one sunny morning by taking snapshots of the children and me standing on the schoolhouse steps. I chose the best and went to a camera shop in Linden and had eight enlargements made. Each night I had worked at making decorative mats for frames and on the Friday that we would get out for Christmas holidays, I brought them, all wrapped, one for each child. When I put them under the tree, I noticed other packages, some wrapped in newspaper, with cards marked in childish sprawl.

We had invited Miss Bunker and Miss Sarah to the Christmas party, but they were not sure they could come. Reverend Milford was to open the party with a reading of the biblical story of Christmas, followed by a prayer. I reminded him that our time would be limited, and he was not offended as he might have been in the early days of our relationship. I would read *The Night Before Christmas* with the children joining in certain parts. By two o'clock, we had finished our work and everything was ready. I thought our tree and decorations were unusually pretty, especially since we had made many of them.

When I opened the front door, a beautiful big car driven by Eddie, with Miss Bunker beside him, pulled into the yard. The car was Miss Bunker's Christmas present to herself, she said with a laugh. They came in loaded with packages, which they, too, put under the tree. Even while we were speaking to them, the door opened and there was Miss Sarah, bringing a box from which floated the aroma of freshly baked cookies. In her other hand was a gallon jug of lemonade. Our party was growing by the minute, and the children were filled with excitement.

Eddie helped Dan and Toby arrange the chairs and benches in a semicircle around the tree while Miss Sarah and I fixed a make-do table for the refreshments. When Reverend Milford arrived, we were ready to begin. I had taught Dimmie to give a welcome. She did it beautifully, and she had practiced saying it without using "ain't." We had all worked on using better grammar.

Miss Bunker said, "We had so much fun at your other party and program that I would not have missed this one."

"Neither would I," said Miss Sarah.

Reverend Milford had a deep, resonant speaking voice, and his reading of the first Christmas was very moving. So was his prayer which, according to promise, he kept short. He was being friendlier to me.

Then I took the book of *The Night Before Christmas*, announcing that the children and I would read it together. In certain parts, I would nod to the children and they joined in perfectly, each having some special lines. Of course, we had arranged that Toby alone would call out the reindeers' names. When it was time for Santa's "goodnight" I pointed to everyone and they joined in.

"Now, Dan, will you give the gifts to Lily and Toby to pass out?" I stood near in case he needed help, but he never did. My gifts consisted of everything from chestnuts and chinquapins to fresh deer and squirrel meat. Ellie, with her mother's help, had baked a pound cake for me, and Debra, a box of chocolate cupcakes. Miss Bunker had given each child a book at his or her reading level, and she had given me a book of Edna St. Vincent Millay's poems. The children were overwhelmed with so many gifts, but I think they liked my photographs best. When the gift giving was over, I asked the older girls to pass out refreshments, the lemonade in jelly glasses as before. The children were delighted with Miss Sarah's cookies cut out in different shapes. Miss Sarah and Miss Bunker loved their wreaths; mine was the prettiest of the lot, and I whispered so to each child. We gave the extra one to Eddie, who had been a great help.

When the party was over, the men and boys arranged the benches and chairs as before and the girls dismantled the tree, putting the ornaments carefully in the box which I surely would not forget to take to Elizabeth. After good-byes were said and only Miss Sarah and Miss Bunker were left, I presented them with my gifts, a watercolor of Miss Sarah's home and one of the schoolhouse for Miss Bunker. They seemed to like them. Then Miss Sarah handed me a box—a fruitcake for Christmas.

When we locked up and said good-bye, Miss Sarah said, "I'll meet you at the Linden depot at three o'clock the Sunday before school reopens."

Again I followed Eddie and Miss Bunker by way of Linden so as to have a better road. When we reached the road where I would turn off, we slowed enough to wave good-bye and to shout "Merry Christmas." I could not understand why, but I had the feeling that this would be the merriest Christmas I had ever had, maybe because Elizabeth and I had tried so hard to make it that way for our family.

16

Christmas at Home

CHRISTMAS WAS WONDERFUL JUST AS WE EXPECTED. I thought it was just as well that none of my friends got home for the holidays that year because it gave me more time with my family. Elizabeth's friend Owen Baker guided us deep into the woods where the holly trees were so thick and loaded with berries that we did not think one would be missed and chose one for our Christmas tree. Owen's sister Mildred helped, and we came home loaded with greenery that made the house look festive. Little Wee was overjoyed with the tree, and this year she did not pull off the ornaments. Rather, she touched them carefully with one finger and was cautious of the prickly holly leaves.

At night we gathered around the piano to sing carols or went serenading to friends, especially to Mrs. Eppes, who always warmed us with hot chocolate. Of course, we missed the jolly Christmases of Egypt and the fun of the Negros trying to catch us in a game called "Christmas gift." That meant upon seeing us on Christmas morning, if they called the words

Christmas gift before we did, we had to give them a gift. They always won, and we had the gifts ready. We agreed not to think back or to mention those jolly days. Besides, we were having a good time, and with the safes on the back porch so heavily stocked with cakes, pies, and other goodies, we had parties as usual. Yes, it was a good Christmas in spite of our father's financial losses.

Although a cold spell was predicted, we were blessed with a few days of sunshine, and one morning Mamma took Wee out in the yard to get the benefit of it. Rosa was not there to help us with our youngster because she was spending a few days with her family, so I put on my coat and went out to give Mamma a hand. While we were there, a buggy pulled up to the gate and out climbed Uncle Reuben and Mammy Lou. Those two never traveled together, and it brought to our minds the same question.

We wondered what had happened to Aunt Deanna and Uncle Cajer. But we did not ask, waiting for them to explain. "Come in and get warm," invited my mother after we had exchanged cheery greetings.

"Miss Lucy, you stil got dat big ol' kitchen range?" asked Uncle Reuben.

"Oh, yes, I couldn't do without that."

"Den ah sho' crave to set by it to git wa'm and to drink some o' yo' good coffee lak ol' times."

"There is a fire in the stove and the coffee is hot; come in and have some."

"We got bad news, but ah needs to set fust," said Mammy Lou with a groan. "Ah got a mis'ry in ma hip."

They sat around the stove while I served the coffee. We waited patiently, feeling that we knew the nature of the bad news.

"Miss Lucy," said Mammy Lou, "dis week us buried bot' Cage and Deanna."

"Both of them!" exclaimed my mother. "I wish we had known. How did it happen?"

"You knows dat Cage been po'ly a long time. He jes quit breathin' one day, jes lak goin' to sleep."

"And Aunt Deanna?" my mother asked.

"She tried to come to de buryin' but she wa'nt able. Hit wuz her heart. De nex' night, she went too."

"Oh, I'm so sorry," said my mother.

"Don' grieve," said Uncle Reuben. "Hit wuz de bes' thing fo' dem. But we sho misses 'em."

"Where are they buried?"

"Right under dem trees whah us used tah set. Us all wants to be buried dare."

"Did Uncle Cajer suffer?"

"No'm, and now Miss Lucy, Cage done daid. Les' let 'im res'." Evidently Mammy Lou did not want to discuss the deaths further. So my mother talked of more cheerful things while I fixed both old people a plate of food which I knew they would enjoy. They ate slowly, pausing to answer my mother's questions. When finished, they rose to go.

"Can't you stay longer?" my mother asked. "My husband would like to see you."

"Dem roads pow'ful bad," said Uncle Reuben. "Mos places us had ter go thu de pas'ters an dat takes time so us needs teh git goin' an git home fo dak."

"Take this lap robe to keep your legs warm," said my mother, picking up one that we used in the buggy in especially cold weather.

"Miss Lucy, dis yo' good lap robe. You mought need hit," said Mammy Lou.

"No, we won't be going out much until the weather is warmer. We'll be coming to see you as soon as we can get over the roads. You take care now, and by the way, is there anything you need?"

"No'm, us got 'nuf. Plenty o' chickens, meat in de smokehouse, meal, flouh, coffee, sorgum lasses fo sweetnin' an' plenty collards in de gauden," Mammy Lou assured us.

"An' ma son done chop us plenty wood fo' de col' weatheh," added Uncle Reuben.

This was the last time we saw Uncle Reuben because he died in January. Mammy Lou lived for several years, and we were relieved when her son and daughter-in-law moved in with her so that she would not be alone. My parents went to see her as long as we lived there.

We enjoyed the holidays, and they went by almost too fast. On the Sunday before the opening of school, the day dawned misty and very cold. The clouds hung low, making the church bell sound loud and clear, almost as if it were right in the house with us. As usual, we had had our baths in zinc tubs the night before, some in front of fires where the water was heated in kettles hanging from cranes, and others behind the big range in the kitchen. In any case, water had to be carried from the well and discarded later and the tubs scrubbed. All of this was quite a chore, and it was understandable that in such weather, most of our daily baths were made before our washstands where we had bowls, pitchers, and slop jars. It was much too cold to consider the shower I had invented on the back porch.

For the first time we donned our new sweaters and the skirts Mamma had made for us. Rosa had one, too, and she was ready when her friend Sam came by as usual to take her to their church.

That Christmas Rosa told us of their impending marriage. "When?" we all asked. We hated to lose Rosa.

"Not soon!" she laughed. "We got to fix up a house first."

Little Wee was very proud of her new snowsuit and kept running to the long hall mirror to look at herself. We laughed at her, and I said, "Mamma, do you think she is going to grow up vain?"

"Oh, no, you all did that way in front of that same mirror whenever you had on a new outfit." Mamma had always made most of our clothes, and I don't think she ever enjoyed anything more than she did sewing for her three little girls.

At church time, sleet had begun to fall, but the church was such a short distance that we walked as usual. The Methodist church, now attended by all denominations in the village, was a large and regal building—the oldest church in Marengo County. The building was completed in 1858, the same year our great-great-grandmother Blount had completed our family home. She was a very religious person, and although there were always religious services for the slaves in their quarters, this grandmother brought to church with her any slave who wished also to attend the white people's services. When I was a child, a few old black people still came on "preaching Sunday," and I later wondered if this were a carryover from olden times. I remember that the white people would shake hands with these black folks to make them welcome.

I think it is not given to the young to reminisce, yet that church held certain memories for me. I always remembered how, as a small child, at night services I slept, stretched out on a bench, my head in my mother's lap; how proud I was when Louie Allen and I were chosen to lead the grand march in the Easter pageant; and how, in that same pageant, my sister Elizabeth and Ev' Peacock passed the collection plates and, to the amusement of all, passed them into all the vacant seats as well just as they had practiced.

Now, more than sixty years later, I get letters from Marengo County relatives saying that the old church, like everything else in the village, is going out of existence, and I do not want to believe it. So I turn back the years again to that Sunday so long ago, when I was the tender age of eighteen and sat listening to my father's beautiful voice, in tune with Mrs. Eppes's old pump organ, and felt confident that whatever else changed, that old church with all that I loved there would endure forever.

After church that day, we did not linger to talk with friends as usual but hurried home. When my father squinted at the sky and said, "We might have snow," he had me worried. At three o'clock we were to meet Miss Sarah at the old Linden depot. Though one of the Coats boys promised to drive for us, snow might make a difference. But one way or another, I had to get there.

Rosa was home, had the table set, and while she and Mamma put dinner on, Daddy helped Elizabeth and me load the car with my suitcases and books. We had agreed that I would not come home on weekends until weather and roads were better.

The trip to Linden was slow because visibility was poor and the isinglass curtains were a poor shield against the winter winds. Rain, mixed with sleet, was falling, and the hand windshield wiper could not keep ice off the glass. As usual in such weather, we had to get out frequently and scrape it off. But we made it, half frozen. We found Miss Sarah already at the depot, poking the fire in the rusty potbellied stove that heated the waiting room. Her cherry greeting helped warm us, and the old stove was a welcome sight in spite of the acrid odor of tobacco and cigarette butts that littered its base. As soon as the chill was off, we transferred my belongings to Miss Sarah's car.

My parting words to Elizabeth were, "Make Daddy bundle up going to the store, and all of you take care, and don't let Mamma work too hard."

"You, too," she said, and we were off in separate directions.

As soon as we were on our way, Miss Sarah held up her finger to show a sparkling new ring.

"Oh, Miss Sarah! From him?"

"Who else?"

For some time, she had had visits from a bachelor who lived in Mississippi; we all liked him.

"I'm so happy for you. When is the wedding?"

"Oh, we haven't set the date yet." Then she sighed. "It's so hard to leave those old people."

"I know."

"But there is one comforting thought. His house has a nice little apartment in back that his mother occupied during her last years. He wants my parents to move there."

"Will they?"

"In time, maybe. I want them to retire, but they are so darn stubborn."

"Aren't they all," I replied.

When we were almost to the school, Miss Sarah pulled off the road on the opposite side and stopped at a gap made in their pasture fence.

"The road is so boggy that we'll go this way through the pasture, hitting the high places." And that is what we did. "For a while, I'll take you to and from school this way."

"Miss Sarah, I am a lot of trouble."

"None at all. You are company for us."

We had a delicious "welcome back" dinner and a short chat by the fire afterward, but we all went to bed early because we had big days ahead.

As we drove through the pasture the next morning, I could see the children darting in and out of the front schoolhouse door. They were looking for me to come down the road as usual. When we reached the gap, Miss Sarah blew the horn and they came running over.

When we got the gap open, the children and I hugged each other. We did not stop to think whether it was the right decorum—we just did it!

"I'm so glad to see you." They did not answer, but their joyous greeting was in their faces.

"Watch for me at three o'clock," called Miss Sarah as she drove away.

As usual, the children wanted to carry everything, and Dan led the way, showing us how to avoid the mud holes. On the porch a lean hound, shaking with the cold, greeted us with a wag of his tail.

"Your dog?" I asked Dan.

"No'm. We never saw 'im before."

"He seems so cold; let's see if he wants to come in, but don't touch him until we know more about him." The dog followed us in and stretched out in the warmth of the stove.

The children deposited my things on the desk, and after hanging our coats on the hooks we sat around the stove, where they had arranged benches. For a few moments we just sat and looked at each other. I realized how much I had missed them. Toby broke the silence.

"Miss Susie, you got on a new sweater 'n' all, but you got on dem same fanger rings."

"And you have a new shirt, don't you? Did your mother make it?"

"She makes all ou' clothes."

"See my new dress?" Debra said timidly. "I'm learning to sew."

"You are! I think that's wonderful. How many of you girls can sew?" Several hands went up, among them Minnie's. She seemed very happy, and I wondered how things were with her. But I thought it best not to ask until we were alone. I was relieved that she was there at all.

"Dan, it is so nice coming into a warm school. Thank you for making this fire."

He frowned. "I-I-I'm afeared the coals done give out. An' the wood's low too. So m-m-many of us has had the flu."

"Oh, I'm sorry." Ellie held up her hand. "Yes, Ellie?"

"Pa knows about the coal. He says he'll get some this week. He's comin' to pick us up in the wagon today and he'll tell you."

"Good," I said. "I have money for coal. Now before we get down to lessons, I'd like to hear what you did during the holidays. Toby, you tell us first."

"Jus befo' Christmas, we went to Demopolis to see the toys. They wuz pretty. That's all we done."

Now Minnie timidly held up her finger for me to see her new ring. The children snickered.

"How pretty, Minnie. From Cluster?"

"Yes'm," she said, blushing. "Pa lets him come to see me, now."

"Minnie, I'm so glad." I breathed a sigh of relief; it was what I had hoped for.

"What did you do, Lily?"

"We had a Christmas tree. Cluster brought it." Now Dimmie and Cammie Milford joined in. "We made things for the tree," said Cammie. "I liked stringin' the popcorn best."

"And Minnie drew things for us," interrupted Dimmie in her enthusiasm. "Bells, an' dolls, n' things; we painted 'em."

"And we painted sweet gum balls like we done here," said

Minnie. Pa went to Linden and bought candy and apples and oranges."

"I'm very, very proud of you. Are your parents well now, Debra?"

"No'm, not 'zactly. Sister says they must stay in a while."

I noticed all of them looking at the rafter where our little mouse used to come. I looked too, and Dan read my thoughts.

"I'm afeared somein' happened to the mouse," he said. "I came twict to feed it but the crumbs are still there." (I made a mental note that Dan was talking better.)

"Maybe it was just time for the mouse to find some companions," I told them. I did not suggest that a hawk or an owl could have caught it. "Are you all ready to do some lessons? We have to work hard to finish our books before school is out in April."

I assigned their lessons and then sat down with Toby. I had a new hard primer that he had not seen. He was enthusiastic.

"This is a hard book, ain't it?" he exclaimed.

"Yes, but I think you can do it; and now that you are growing up, you should work on talking better too. Try to say, 'isn't it,' not 'ain't it.'"

"I'll try." Maybe we should all work on that, I thought.

During the holidays, Mr. Dick had told me that it was in the planning to improve the road, making it possible for these children to go by bus to Linden the next year, but he did not want to announce it until they were certain. The thought struck me that when they took the county examinations for grade placement, they might not pass.

Oh, dear! I thought. I cannot let that happen! Maybe I should put more pressure on them. Then I knew I could not do that. They had so many strikes against them—irregular schooling, a short school year, and now, in me, a teacher with no experience. But with Miss Bunker's help, I knew that I was better now than I was in the beginning. We would go on as we had. They were all doing their best.

At recess time, it was much too cold to play outside, and, besides, the yard was very muddy. They had learned to love games and were disappointed.

"We'll play an indoor game," I consoled them. "Did you ever play 'huckle-buckle bean stalk'?" They had not, so I explained.

"One of us will be 'it.' While the others close their eyes, that one who is 'it' will take some object—the eraser will do—and hide it. It must be where it can be seen but not too plainly. When the hider says, 'ready,' all wander around, looking. The first one who sees the eraser says, 'Huckle-buckle bean stalk.' Then he or she gets to hide 'it.'" They got into the spirit, even Dan, and not only did we have fun, but we got some exercise.

When lunchtime came and we got out our food, the old hound woke up and sniffed.

"I think he is half starved," I said looking at his ribs. "My mother made me too many sandwiches so I'll give him one and then we can give him any scraps."

The sandwich disappeared like magic. "I'll get him some water," said Minnie.

"I suppose we have ourselves a new pet," I said, watching the old hound go around to each person and beg for more.

"He does not have a collar, and if he stays, we must get rabies shots for him as soon as the roads allow us to take him to Linden." In those days a "mad dog" was a frightening thing, and we could not risk his having rabies.

When the school day was over and it was time for Miss Sarah, I looked at the hound. "I surely hate to turn him out in such weather. If we only had something to make him a bed under the house."

Dan spoke up. "That big pasteboard box that you brought things in onct is still under there with the kindling. I'll put it under the flo' where the stove sets. I'll bank the fire with ashes and it will be kind o' wa'm there." Dan crawled under the house and pulled the box to the right spot, and the children helped pile the kindling around it to keep off the wind.

Just then Mr. Douglas drove up in his wagon. "Hidy, Miss Susie. What yaw'l doin?" he asked as he walked around to where we were.

"We have a dog that has taken up with us. Do you know to whom he belongs, Mr. Douglas?" He took a good look at the hound.

"He don't belong aroun' here. Was probably lost in a coon or possum hunt." Mr. Douglas squatted down and looked at the bed the children were making.

"I've got a' old blanket in the wagon—not much good—get it, Toby." The bed looked inviting, and the hound crawled in and laid down.

"Come in the house, Mr. Douglas. I want to give you the money Mr. Dick sent for the coal."

"I go tomorrow," he said, "and I'll pick up all the children after school. It won't do for them to walk in this weather with so much flu aroun'."

"Oh, Mr. Douglas, you are so kind."

Miss Sarah's horn blew. "Dan, you'll bank the fire and lock up, won't you?"

I put on my wraps and said good-bye. As I hurried across the road to join Miss Sarah, I had the happy feeling, tinged with a little sadness, that we were on our way to the last term taught in that little one-room school.

17

The Runaway

S USUAL, THE PENNEYS HAD A GOOD SUPPER, BUT
Miss Sarah did not join us. She took an aspirin and
went to bed, saying she did not feel well. Her parents were in a dither, and during supper they
took turns running in to feel her forehead or to take her a cool
drink. Mr. Penney ran a little store out by the road, and Mrs.
Penney claimed their small dairy as her project, but actually
Miss Sarah ran them both and everything they undertook, and
when she could not function, neither could they. She was a
spinster of thirty-some years, but she was their heart, and they
still called her "baby."

After one of Mrs. Penney's trips to Miss Sarah's bedroom,
she said to me: "Baby says you must not come in there because
she thinks she has the flu. We'll get your things out and you
sleep in the other room. If you get sick, the school would have
to close."

"Oh, I had not thought of that!" Except for the polio attack, I had led a healthy life, and I was not afraid of any illness, but the school closing was an alarming thought.

When both Mr. and Mrs. Penney were at the table, I thought I should give them a word of caution.

"Don't you think you should be extra careful, too? If one of you got sick Miss Sarah would probably get out of that bed and that would be bad for her."

They looked at each other.

"She is right," said Mrs. Penney. "We must be careful. Papa, maybe you'd better get out the asafetida bags and we can hang them around our necks."

"That evil-smelling stuff," he snorted, but he did as she bade.

I had heard of this old-wives'-tale remedy but had never smelled it. When I took one whiff, I could see why it would keep germs or anything else away, and I heard Miss Sarah scream, "Get away with that concoction. It makes me feel worse."

At seven o'clock the next morning, Mrs. Penney gave a timid knock on the door.

"Miss Susie, you wake?"

"Is it late?" I asked with the alarming thought that I had overslept.

"Oh, no, we just need to talk, and you don't mind if Papa builds up your fire?"

"Of course not, but I could do that."

"Oh, he always attends to the fires."

Just like my father, I thought. He raked off the ashes and laid on fat pine that was soon blazing; then he added coal. Mrs. Penney sat on the side of my bed.

"How is Miss Sarah?" I asked.

"She feels pretty bad. It's flu, all right—chills, aches, and fever; but right now she is worried about your getting to school."

"She shouldn't be worried."

"Well, we'd be glad for you to use the car, but she says she's afraid for you to drive through the pasture as she does because if you didn't hit the hard places just right you'd get stuck as bad as on the road, maybe worse. We were going to send word to Mr. Douglas to pick you up, but some of the cowhands said he passed a good while ago."

"Yes, he told me he was bringing the children to school real early because he is going to Demopolis for a ton of coal today. Maybe this is the day I should ride the horse."

"Maybe so—but it's awfully cold, and I hate for you to ride that horse. The cowhands say he is all right, but he's young and has never had a lady on him."

"Don't you worry, Mrs. Penney. This lady," I teased, "is used to riding; I'm glad I brought my riding habit."

"Honey, you talking 'bout them pants?"

"Yes ma'am." I pulled the riding habit out of the closet. "See, it has a long coat with it."

"Chile, you can't teach in pants. Folks would talk."

At that moment, the cook came in with a tray. There was a steaming cup of coffee and cream so thick I had to lift it with a spoon.

"How good this tastes."

"Honey, you ain't got a skirt you could ride in, have you?" asked Mrs. Penney.

"No, I didn't bring one."

The cook was going out the door. She paused, then came back. "Miss Susie, you wantin' somen' to ride in?" she asked.

"Yes, I wish I'd borrowed one o' these divided ridin' skirts."

"Chile, no need o' that. You kin do whut I does when I rides the mule to chetch. I gits on in my reg'lar Sunday dress, then I ties a cook ap'on so's it kivvers one leg, then one on 'tother side to kivver that one. We got plenty ap'ons to lend ya."

Mrs. Penney and I laughed, but it solved the problem.

"Now you get dressed and come to breakfast. I'll fix you a lunch in a basket so's you can carry it on the horse. You dress warm now. You got a wool scarf for your head?"

"Why, no, only a silk one."

"I'll get you one of Sarah's."

When I was ready to leave, one of the cowhands brought the horse around. As I walked toward him, he shied a little.

"Stop that, Scamp," said the man, slapping him with the reins.

"Tell me about him," I asked. My father always said it was important for a rider to know his horse because they have personalities just as people do.

"Oh, Scamp's all right," he said, "just a little skittish. He's feelin' his oats in this cold weather is all, but he's got a tough mouth; you better keep him in check. But I don't think you gotta worry 'cause that road's so deep in mud, he couldn't run if he wanted to."

I got on and picked up the reins. The cook was there with the two aprons. When they were hanging over my legs, I thought I looked modest enough to satisfy anyone, even Reverend Milford.

Mrs. Penney handed up the lunch basket.

"It's got a piece of the Baby's lemon pie in there."

"Well, I surely won't drop that!"

The horse pranced a little. It was plain that he wanted to run, but I kept a tight rein, and when we got out in the road the mud slowed him down. His feet went down a foot in the mire and he pulled them out with a sucking noise.

I could hear hogs squealing at the farmhouse to our right. It was plain that they were having hog killing. One of the frightened animals got out of the pen and ran in our direction, making a wolf-wolf-wolfing sound, a man close on his heels.

I was in sympathy with the hog because since childhood I had hated to see them butchered. The hog, running fast, gained ground and made straight for us. My mount was so intent on his footing that he did not see the panic-stricken animal until it plunged into the road, right under us. Now Scamp reared and was making every effort to run. I could feel his muscles doubling up under me, churning, churning. The road was especially low here, and there were banks on either side. Then I saw it—a path leading up to one of the banks, but alas, Scamp saw it before I did, and he made for it. With all my strength, I pulled the reins in the opposite direction, but he was determined and went up the path sideways. With only the open road ahead, we now took off. I had had many a swift ride on my little horse Clark when we lived on Egypt, but Clark was always under control. This horse was not! As we hit the wind, it got under the aprons so that they flew back and whipped him on the rear, adding to his panic, I'm sure. I could only hope he was surefooted because though the path was fairly hard, there were mud holes, slick places, and, worst of all, clumps of last year's dead blackberry vines, all of which could trip a horse. He cleared them all.

I did not have much time to consider my appearance, but I do recall thinking that as we neared the school I must have resembled a partially clad Lady Godiva gone wild. I had lost Miss Sarah's head scarf, leaving my long hair, like the aprons, to blow back in the wind; my stockings were down and my dress up to my homemade teddies, leaving my legs and thighs completely bare. In this fashion we sailed past the school.

Out of the corner of my eye, I could see Dan bringing in wood. I thought I heard him utter an exclamation that brought other children to the porch. I could only imagine the looks of horror on their faces at seeing their teacher go by in such a manner.

Now another disastrous thought entered my mind. In a few miles, we would come to the Linden-Demopolis highway, where a collision with traffic was possible unless I could check our speed. I had an idea: if I could only pull in the aprons that would no doubt allay the horse's fears a little. The lunch basket was over my right arm so I transferred both reins to that hand, leaving my left hand free. I did not hold on with my hands anyway. Good riders held with their knees, and mine were tightly glued to the saddle. (I could only hope we had a strong girth.) Now, by reaching back with my left hand, I managed to tuck first one, then the other apron under me. I felt a ray of hope that the horse would begin to slow down, when, horror of horrors, ahead was the Reverend Milford, who no doubt, like Mr. Douglas, was afraid of the flu epidemic and was bringing his children to school in an old mule-drawn wagon. Of all the people in the world, Reverend Milford was the last one I wanted to see me as I was.

I attempted a dignified, "Hi-do" as I sped by and I caught a glimpse of his wide-eyed look of astonishment. I went around a curve but not before hearing Reverend Milford's loud "Whoa" and the screech of his wagon wheels scraping the bed. He was turning around to follow me and pick up the pieces.

Then ahead I saw a welcome sight. Some men were moving their herd of cattle from one pasture across the road to the other. The cattle completely blocked our path.

"Oh Lord," I prayed. "Please keep them there."

The cows might have scattered before a runaway horse, but the men, sensing the situation, spread out across the road.

"Whoa, boy, whoa," one man called out, and perhaps because Scamp recognized the authority to which he was accustomed, he halted momentarily. The man then made a dash for the horse and grabbed the reins.

"Quick, help the lady down," he said to the man nearest, and although Scamp reared, the man pulled me from his threatening hooves. I welcomed his assistance. I was trembling, but Scamp was trembling more. He was foaming at the mouth and panting for breath.

"Miss, what you doing on such a horse, and in this weather?"

"I'm the schoolteacher above here. I was trying to get to school."

"Well, ma'am, no one should have allowed you on this horse. How you stayed on I don't know."

"I could have managed but something scared him."

"Well, ma'am, I'm jes glad we wus here."

"Me too," I smiled weakly.

Reverend Milford came around the curve. He was laying the whip on his mule and had it in full gallop. He pulled up beside us and climbed out while the children sat there wide-eyed. Of course, Lily was sobbing.

"Miss Susie, you hurted? Did you fall off?"

"No, sir, Reverend Milford, these kind men stopped the horse."

Reverend Milford recognized the men and introduced us.

"This is the Penneys' horse, ain't it?" he asked. "How come him to run away, Miss Susie?"

"Why, a pig ran under him and then these aprons." They were entangled around my waist, and I began to pull them off.

Reverend Milford, bringing his children to school

"Aprons?" asked the Reverend.

"See," I said, "the cook showed me how to make a riding skirt out of them—only—only when the horse ran, they flew back and whipped him on the back."

Then I began to laugh and cry at the same time. Reverend Milford began to laugh, more out of relief than humor, and so did the men. Only the children still sat there wide-eyed and could not laugh.

"I know you're half froze," said Reverend Milford. "Let's get to the school and get you warm. Thank you fellows again."

I did not know how to thank those people who saved my life, which they probably did, so I just waved.

They had tied Scamp behind the wagon, and he seemed content to follow the mule.

Minnie and the other girls sat on quilts in the bottom of the wagon, leaving the seat for their father and me. Lily crawled onto her father's lap for comfort. For the first time, I began to know this rough old preacher for the good friend that he was to become.

"Reverend Milford," I said when we were on our way, "I'm sorry for the spectacle I made. I truly am."

He looked at me a long time. "Miss Susie, all's important is you're all right. You ain't hurted. Here you only a girl, an' you doin' a woman's job, an doin' it good. When I think how you come out in this weather, ridin' a runaway hoss, to teach our younguns—why, Miss Susie, I can't"—he couldn't say more. He wiped his nose on his rough sleeve and in his eyes there were tears. I couldn't keep back the tears either.

"Miss Susie, I didn't 'preciate you at first, but I do now."

"Oh, thank you, Reverend. You're so good," and I really believed it.

So with the winter winds howling around us and Reverend Milford urging the mule onward, we bumped along slowly in the old wagon, its wobbly wheels making crazy tracks in the frost-crusted mud as it carried us slowly to our little school.

18

Out of Fuel
in a Snowstorm

WHEN THE RICKETY OLD WAGON BEARING REVerend Milford, his children, and me pulled into the schoolyard, the pupils waiting there were off the porch and trying to help us even before the mule came to a halt. They all seemed anxious to touch me, to see if I was real and in one piece. They began to pepper me with questions:

"Did you fall off?"

"Are you all right?"

"How'd you stop that hoss?"

"Now! Now!" scolded Reverend Milford. "What ails you chillun? Can't you see yo' teacher is half froze an' shook up from that ride? Quit pesterin' her!"

"It's all right, Reverend Milford," I said, trying to talk with my teeth chattering. "They are just anxious. Children, let me get warm, then we'll talk."

We started up the steps, Toby clasping my hand as he had on the first day of school.

"Wait, Miss Susie," said Reverend Milford, untying Scamp. "What we gonna do with this hoss? One thing fo' certain—you ain't gonna ride him agin, are ye?"

"Oh, no, sir! The Penneys said I was to put him through the gap to their pasture."

"Where?" he began, looking toward the fence.

"I know," said Dan. "I'll he'p."

"And Dan," I called as they led the horse away, "please bring in the bridle and saddle."

The children pulled my chair close to the potbellied old stove that was radiating warmth, then they crowded around while Toby sat at my feet, still tightly grasping my hand. I tried to talk to them, but my teeth were still chattering and the words would not come out. Debra was the first to understand, then Minnie.

"We'll find something to do," said Debra, giving the other children a nudge. Debra had more wisdom for her years than most children.

Lily still needed help and clung to Minnie, who said, "Come, Lily. I want to hear you read."

I gave Minnie a grateful smile, then turned to Debra.

"Will you please let Toby continue with his number workbook? After I rest, I'll introduce him to the first reader, which he is so anxious to try."

Dimmie stood there, looking wistful. I felt that she needed a challenge, too. "Dimmie," I said, "would you like to be teacher for Cammie and Ellie until I get warm? They can show you their assignments." She looked so happy that I wondered why I had not had the insight to give her some such responsibilities before.

Just then the front door opened and Reverend Milford and

Dan entered, bringing a blast of cold air. Dan was excited. Now he stuttered as he had when I first knew him.

"L-l-look out," he said pointing to the windows. "S-s-see, it's s-s-snowin'."

The children, who were just settling down to work, dropped everything and ran to the windows. It had been several years since we had a real snow in our part of Alabama. Except for a few flakes now and then, Toby had never seen snow.

Now all eyes were turned to the gray clouds and the falling flakes. Only the wet, sputtering wood in the stove broke the silence. A deep snow would only add to our transportation problems. I realized that, but I was young and the prospect of the beauty and excitement that a snow would bring was over-whelming. I wanted the children to experience it.

I was so engrossed in memories of other snows that I almost forgot about Reverend Milford, who was standing by me, holding out his rough, knotty hands to the heat of the stove. He was shivering, and his face was very red.

"Reverend Milford," I said. "Do you feel well?"

"No'm, I can't say as I do. I'm afeared I'm comin' down with somen', but that ain't wut's worryin' me. I been lookin' in the back yard. Miss Susie, you not only outa coal, these few sticks o' wood on the flo' is all you got. We had so much sickness during Christmas, we didn't notice you wuz so low."

Dan heard and came to join us. "I got a ax. There's one lil' log left. I'll go cut it up."

I patted Dan on the arm. "With this fine boy to help us, we'll get by until Mr. Douglas comes with the coal. Now you go home, Reverend Milford, and get in bed. You can't fool around with flu, which you may be taking."

"But you been through so much today, Miss Susie, maybe I had ought to take you home first."

"Oh, no, I'm going to teach. Mr. Douglas will take me home. He told Ellie that he is going to take all the children home today, also."

"He is? Then I'll tell the Tuckers when I go by. They been so sick they hadn't ought to be out in this weather neither. Well, I reckon I'll go."

We could hear Reverend Milford drive away, and Dan went out with the ax. Now the snow was falling thicker, making spirals in the wind. The children were enthralled with the wonder of it so I did not disturb them. I leaned back in my chair and closed my eyes. I could faintly hear Dan chopping wood. Other than that, nothing disturbed the peace and stillness of that little schoolroom, and I felt fortunate to be a part of it. I felt especially fortunate to be teaching eight such wonderful children. Finally, I could hear them tiptoeing, one by one, back to their seats to begin their assignments. I was becoming warm and drowsy, a good time for reflection.

I had taught the children a little over four months now, and I wondered if I, as a teacher, had given them all that I should. As far as subject matter was concerned, with Miss Bunker's help, possibly I had. In other ways I was not so sure. My own teachers of whom I had the fondest recollections were those who gave me something greater than the knowledge contained between the covers of books. I was not quite sure what that something was. There were moments when I thought we had touched on it, as on our autumn walks; in our Thanksgiving party, when we felt, as never before, a closeness to the parents and the community; in our shared love of animals, first the mouse and now the hound; and in our present sharing of the wonders of a snowfall. There were two months ahead of us, and then spring would come. Oh, spring! If I could only help them feel the magic of it!

I was drawn out of my reverie by Dan's attempts to ease down an armload of wood quietly so as not to disturb me. I opened my eyes.

"Oh, Miss Susie," he apologized. "I d-didn't mean to wake you."

"You didn't. I was just resting. I see you did get some wood. I'm glad."

He looked worried and said, "I-I'm afeared tain't much good. The l-log wuz rotten."

"Well, it will help. But this snow, if it gets deep, might delay Mr. Douglas. Dan, what do you think of just putting one stick on the fire at a time?"

"Yes'm, it would last longer, and we could turn the damper down but t'wouldn't give out m-much heat."

"Well, we could put on all our wraps and sit close to the stove." All too soon, this was what we had to do. The children were having trouble concentrating. Finally, I suggested we put work away and just talk a while. They all liked this because we seldom had time for such things.

Although I had adhered to Mr. Dick's wishes not to discuss the news that by the following year the children would be taken to Linden by bus, word had gotten around and I felt sure they had heard it; therefore, I asked them point-blank. Yes, all had heard.

"But I want to stay here with you," said Toby, leaning his head against my knee.

"I won't be here after this year, Toby, and besides, I think you will like a big school. You'll have many children to play with, more things to do, ball games, and a lot of fun." He shook his head and seemed to concentrate on the snow that was now piling against the windowpanes. Whereas earlier it had seemed beautiful and friendly, now it appeared threatening.

"I'm not going to Linden," said Minnie. "Ma an Pa have promised that if I finish the eighth grade with you, me an' Cluster can git married."

"Well, Minnie," I said. "In your case, maybe that is the thing to do. You have found a fine boy. He is making a home for you, and you both seem to know what you want."

"I'm glad you feel thataway," she said. "I could'n stand it if you wuz agin me, Miss Susie."

"What about you, Dan?" I think I worried most about him. He tried so hard.

"Miss Susie, I-I don' know. I would like to finish high school, but Pa ain't so well. Peers lak I might have to stop school an' he'p 'im."

"But you are just starting the dairy you hope to have some-day, aren't you?"

"Yes'm. I got two pretty heifers of my own a'ready."

"It's good to have a start on what you want to do with your life."

"I know for sure what I want to do," said Debra. "When I finish high school, my sister, the nurse, is going to get me in nursing school. When I finish that and get to making money, I'm gonna he'p Ma an' Pa an' maybe Dan, too."

"And I know you will, Debra. And Dimmie, do you know what you want?"

"Yes'm. I want to be a schoolteacher, like you. I reckon that 'pends on effen I kin git money to go on to school."

"If you keep making such good grades and try hard, there may be people to help you."

Cammie, my little clown, spoke up. "I want to do like Dimmie—be a teacher—if I kin."

"You try hard and you'll do it, I know. And you, Ellie?"

"I wanna get married an' have a lotta chillun."

"You'll make a good mother." She was always mothering Toby. "If you go on to school a while you'll learn so many things, among them how to be a better mother. Don't you think so?"

"I don't know, ma'am. I guess so."

"I promise you, you will." Ellie showed me one of her nicest smiles. She was so pretty that I felt sure when she grew up there would be many suiters asking for her hand in marriage. Then I turned to my youngest girl—my dear, insecure little Lily.

"Lily, what would you like to do?"

"I want to go to school in the daytime and live with Ma and Pa at night. I don't want to ever leave 'em."

"And I know they feel that way about you, too. You keep making good grades, and they will always be proud of you. In fact, they are proud of you just as you are."

"They are?" She smiled timidly and eased over until she stood close to me. It seemed that Lily needed more than I was giving her. I made a mental note that I must talk to her parents to help them better understand her needs. I wondered if her mother and father knew what those needs were or what had caused Lily's deep feeling of insecurity.

I felt Toby squeeze my hand. He looked up with his winning smile.

"Did you forget me?" he asked.

"Why, Toby! I'd never forget you. We are all anxious to know what you want to be when you grow up." He stood up and stretched, then he puffed out his chest and stood as tall as he could.

"I want to be a lot of things—a cowboy an' a fireman an'

more. We wuz in Demopolis onct an' the fire engines went by. They wuz goin' fas'."

"How are you going to learn to be all of these things?" I asked.

"Why, you know, get a ed-ju-ca-shun. That's what my Ma and Pa say."

"Why, Toby, you and I are a lot alike. That's what I'm trying to do, get an education."

"Oh you a'ready know evything, Miss Susie—doncha?"

"Oh, no, Toby. There is a big world out there full of wonderful things. I want to see and do them all—at least as much as I can. Do you know, you can do almost anything you wish—if you try hard enough."

Now Minnie hung her head. "I guess I'll never know about them things—effen I git married, that is, I won't know nuthin much."

"That's where you are wrong, Minnie. At first, you can just read about the world. If you live near a library, that would be nice. But if you don't, then get Cluster to take some boards and make a bookcase for you. Get a mail order catalog, and when you have a little money to spare, order a book now and then. I'll make a list for you. And I also have a few books I can spare. Dan, you can do the same. And who knows—someday you may be able to travel to many of the places you read about. When we study about one of our presidents, Abraham Lincoln, you'll see what a hard time he had getting an education, but he got it."

I decided then and there that I must read them the story of this president's life. More than ever, I realized that these children had a seriousness of purpose beyond their years.

I was beginning to feel numb, and the muscles strained during the ride that morning was becoming a little sore. "Let's stand up a while. Maybe we should look out the windows to see what the snow is doing." Now the flakes were falling so thick that they were covering the ground and making pretty designs out of the cotton stalks.

"You can't hardly see the woods no mo', can ya?" observed Toby.

"That's right, Toby. I think you are going to see a real snow. It'll be deep by tomorrow, I think, and we can have some fun." I wanted to keep fearful thoughts of being snowbound out of their heads.

"How?" they all wanted to know.

"Why, we'll make a snowman and play snowball, and if we bring the things for it, we can make snow ice cream." We agreed that Ellie and Toby would bring a jar of fresh cream, Debra would bring vanilla, and the Milfords and I would bring the sugar. I could borrow from Mrs. Penney a large spoon and dishpan. In our enthusiasm, I noticed that the problem of our diminishing fuel seemed to be forgotten for the moment—that is, by all except Dan. He picked up the largest stick and laid it on the few remaining coals. Then he left the stove door open, and the soft reflections of the flames lit up the faces of the children. It gave a deceiving look of warmth, but at least it added a cheeriness we had not had before. Dan spoke up.

"I feel like I'm to blame for lettin' the wood give out. You know, I been taking that five dollars a month fo' keeping the house warm."

"Oh, Dan, never think that," I insisted. "It couldn't be helped with flu in all your families. Besides, Mr. Douglas may be here soon."

There were only three sticks left. "Maybe I kin fin' somen' to cut up," he said. I followed him to the back door and we looked out.

"Dan, if you didn't see anything before, you won't now. See, everything is covered with snow."

"We might could spare one bundle of kindlin'," he said.

"Well, bring one in, but only one because the coal won't do us any good without that." I went back to the children; I was feeling better.

"Now, let's get on with some work," I said. "Let's sit as close as we can to the stove, and here is your assignment. Your stories about our falling in the creek were so good that I want you to try to do an even better one about the snow. This way we'll learn spelling, penmanship, and English all in one lesson. This time, Toby, you are on your own. I'll give you any help you need on the spelling and printing; you do the same, Lily." This assignment was a challenge, but it was to their liking. Dan especially went about it with determination. Except in number work, he was not up to grade level, but in every written assignment he showed that he had a greater appreciation of aesthetics than all the others.

The room was very quiet during the assignment, the silence broken only when I helped them. When the last child had finished, it was lunchtime.

"Before we read our stories, would you like to eat lunch?" They were ready, and, as usual, our hound stirred from his place nearest the stove and began to beg. When I opened my lunch basket, I was not surprised to see that the meringue pie was scattered around in bits but still edible. What I enjoyed most, however, was a sweet potato, roasted in its jacket, that had been sent by Mrs. Tucker. I laid it on the stove to get warm. When we had all finished and the old hound had been given the scraps, Toby had an idea.

"Kin I git some snow an bring it in so's we kin look at it?"

"Yes, Toby."

"Here, use my paint pan," said Minnie. Toby and Lily went out to get it, and the other children giggled.

"He don't know it's gonna melt," laughed Dan.

They brought the pan in, piled with snow.

"Want to feel it?" asked Toby, passing it around. "It's cold an' wet, and when you hol' some in yo' han, you look an' it ain't there—jus' a wet spot."

Toby set the pan near the stove to warm his hands. When he looked at the snow again, it was fast melting.

"What's it doin', Miss Susie? It's turning to water!"

"You see, Toby, this snow was made when the moisture was a certain temperature up in the atmosphere or the sky, and it will go back to water." Seeing the look of disappointment on his face, I hastened to add, "but it's so cold outside that the snow out there won't melt too quickly."

After this excitement, the children returned to their stories, and, as before, each story revealed much about the writer. I read Toby's aloud for him; his was the most unusual.

Snow

When I wake up I look out thu my Ma's florsak curtins. I can not see good. Snow is that way. The woods look way off an the tres is white. The cotton staks look lik white rabbits. I like snow it is soft and wet like whip cream.

Toby

I complimented all of them. "Four months ago, you could not do so well. I'll take them home to correct because I will have a better light there." The room was becoming so cold and dark that I felt we could not work any more. We jumped around to get warm. Then I got out *Pollyanna* by Eleanor Porter to read to them, but even in front of the flames it was so difficult to see that I gave it up. I looked around for the first time to see if there might be a kerosene lamp on the wall, but there was none. We never expected to be there in the dark.

At four o'clock, we had used our last stick of wood. Dan looked at me helplessly.

"Whut we gonna do now?"

"Dan, come with me to the back of the room." There was an old bench there with one leg missing. We never used it. "Do you think you can chop this up?"

"Yesin, I could. But won't folks be mad?"

"No, I don't think anyone will object to anything we do today to keep warm." He started to take it outside. "It's too cold out there. Try to do it here." As soon as he had some pieces small enough to get in the stove door, we tried it. It burned fine, almost too well, and it gave some heat.

Just then a horse clattered into the yard. Oh, welcome sound! It was Scamp with Butch riding him; Butch tied the horse to the porch post and came in. My relief at seeing him was extreme.

"Mrs. Penney got worried 'bout yawl," he said, "so she sent me to see 'bout ya."

"We're waiting on Mr. Douglas, and now I'm worried about him. We expected him much earlier."

"He's comin'. I could see 'im down the road a ways. An' I'm gonna stay long nuf to he'p him unload the coal."

"Oh, I'm glad because he must be about frozen. By the way, Scamp's saddle an' bridle are back there."

"I hear tell he run away with you," said Butch. "I'm sho' sorry."

"Yes, but how did you know?"

"Oh, ev'ybody 'roun here knows it by now. They tell me you hung on." I nodded. "He ain't never done that befo'!"

"He had reason to run. Oh, here comes Mr. Douglas." Butch and Dan began unloading the coal. Mr. Douglas came up the back steps.

"Pa, you all right?" asked Ellie. She and Toby were pulling him closer. "All 'cept I'm froze," he laughed.

"Mr. Douglas," I said, "this is terrible weather for you to be out."

"Well, it wouldn't been too bad but I couldn't see the road good with the snow n' all, and one wheel hit a hole an' come off. I had to go git help. We had a time. I'd a been back long befo' now 'cept for that."

Now that we had fuel, we piled on more parts of the old bench and Toby brought in a big lump of coal. Soon we had the usual roaring fire. I sank back in my chair with a sigh of relief, and Mr. Douglas sat down, taking my suggestion that the boys finish unloading the coal. I had grown up in big farm-houses, heated with fireplaces, but never before had it felt so good to get warm.

When we were ready to leave, Dan banked our fire to en-sure heat tomorrow. Then he looked at the hound.

"Miss Susie, kin I take 'im home? He might freeze outside."

"Please do, and from now on he is your dog." The other children looked disappointed.

"Oh, I'll bring 'im back ev'y day," he assured them.

Butch had ridden away to tell the Penneys that everything was all right and that Mr. Douglas was bringing us home. We locked the doors and went to the wagon. Snow was blinding us and seeping in around our upturned collars.

"Now," said Mr. Douglas, "I've got two tarps. Ya'll set on

one and pull the t'other all the way over you. That's the onliest way." He lit an old lantern and handed it to Dan. "Dan, you set by me, and maybe with this light, you kin help me see to miss the holes."

The other children and I crowded together under the tarp, along with the hound. When Mr. Douglas tucked the tarp around us, it was as dark as midnight and we laughed at our strange circumstances. It seemed that no sooner had I gotten warm from the first wagon ride than here I was, going for another. As we rattled along in the snowstorm, I felt that never again in my life would I have such an eventful day.

19

We Learn about Birds
and Other Wildlife

THE COLD SPELL OF JANUARY THAT BEGAN WITH the snowstorm lasted for several weeks, with temperatures going down in the teens. Dan kept the potbellied stove red hot at the cost of using much fuel. Mr. Douglas, not wanting to run the risk of running out of coal again, went to Demopolis for more, and Dan, in his free time, worked at restoring the woodpile. The old hound was a part of everything Dan did.

After the fun and excitement of the snow passed, the children spent their spare time poring over the old encyclopedias, given to them by Miss Sarah. Miss Sarah, now up and around, apologized for the dust on the books. I had to laugh at that and told her that if they had been dusty that was a thing of the past because every book in the set was getting much use now.

"I don't know why I did not think of giving those children the books long ago. By the way, when school is out, do you want them?"

"We have some about as old. I was thinking of the Milford

family and how important it would be for their many children to have access to them. I believe Reverend Milford himself would enjoy them, don't you?"

"Yes, but I was thinking of Debra. She is so smart," suggested Miss Sarah.

"There is also Dan. He wants so much to finish high school, and you know the situation there. Now he has to do all the farm work. Let's just wait a while and see who uses the books most."

"Well, you decide. When do you think you will tell them?"

"Not until the end of school. Now the children enjoy feeling that the books belong to all of them, and I'd like to keep it that way. I'll ask whoever is given the books to share them with the other two families."

I felt that because of their enthusiasm, the children were learning more geography and history from the encyclopedias than from their textbooks. They would become interested in a picture of some strange people, scenery, or animal, ask me to help them read the captions, then turn to the globe to find the location. Even Lily and Toby caught the "fever" and began to learn that acquiring knowledge could be exciting.

One day Toby called my attention to a color plate of animals. He took his forefinger and traced the picture of a tiger.

"This is a tiger," he said. "I saw one in a circus onct. He done tricks, but my Pa says they'll eat you up right now if you fool with 'em."

"Well, they can be dangerous, but most of them are not maneaters. They live contented lives in jungles if people leave them alone."

"And they don't all live in circuses?" he asked.

"Oh, no, just a few. But it's kind of cruel, I guess, to do that to animals."

Toby sat there, deep in thought, apparently trying to re-adjust his thinking about the life of wild animals.

The rest of January was cold and rainy, but the first week of February dawned with a sunny splendor that dried up the yard, enabling us to play out-of-doors, sometimes even without wraps. Dan declined to join in our games, saying he needed to continue his work of replenishing the woodpile. Besides, I felt that some of our games were a little childish for him.

Cammie was always looking for a game with more fun in it, and one day when we went out at the noon hour, she said, "I wish we could play a new game, Miss Susie. It'ud pleasure us if you'd teach us one."

"Well, I do think of one we have not played. Long ago, when my grandmother was a little girl, children played many singing games. She used to rock me to sleep singing one Chicken—Ma chicken—Ma Craney Crow.

I taught the children the song and then the game. We were playing it quite well and laughing so hard that we did not see Miss Bunker's car drive into the yard.

"You seem to be having a lot of fun," she said, as she got out. We ran to help her.

"You see, I am learning to drive on these roads," she said.

She and I had talked by phone, but she had not visited our school since before Christmas because of the bad weather. The children took her books, then Lily took one hand and Toby the other. The rest of us followed them up the steps and into the room. The children arranged two chairs for us by the stove and then took our wraps.

"Wait a minute before you set, Miss Bunker," said Toby. "We got some'n' to show ya." He led her to the bookcase. "See, we got us some cy-cy-cydopedas." All of the children crowded around to show her something of interest that they had found, and Dan, having come in, joined them while the hound took his usual warm spot by the stove. Miss Bunker looked at their discoveries with interest and then told them how proud she was of them.

"Now," she said, "I need to talk to your teacher. Is there something else you could do?"

"Children," I said, "you could finish the assignment we started this morning."

As always, they obeyed, but they were reluctant to give up their conversation with Miss Bunker.

"How is everything going?" Miss Bunker asked when we were seated alone.

"As well as possible, I think. We are trying hard to finish our books before school closes."

"Well Susie, we keep trying to get a full nine-month term for this school, but always the same story—no money."

"Word has leaked out about the children going by bus to Linden, and all plan to go except Minnie—and maybe Dan," I told her.

"Why do you think those two will drop out?"

"Well, Minnie is to be married in June. Dan would like to finish high school, but he can only do that if his father's health improves. Lately Dan has had to do all the farm work. He has done well to stay in school so far."

"That's a shame, but he's a fine boy to shoulder so much responsibility."

Miss Bunker spent the afternoon testing each child's level of achievement. I was very anxious to learn the results. She knew this so she told me as much as she could.

"Debra and Toby are well above grade level," she said. "And Dimmie rates high; Cammie, Ellie, and Lily are satisfactory. Considering all their problems, Minnie and Dan do as well as could be expected. I think you should be proud of all their achievements and not worry."

Of course, that was easier said than done, and I did worry.

"Miss Bunker, I do want them to pass the county board tests because they have tried so hard. They are more serious about their schoolwork than most children."

"Perhaps they have caught some of your thirst for knowledge," she said, smiling.

"I hope so. I only wish I could give them half the inspiration that my teachers gave me."

As usual in that part of Alabama, February alternated between warm and cold days. When the sun was unusually bright, we would get the urge to walk to the woods to look for signs of spring. We found cape jasmine blooming, but that was all. It was a very pretty vine with small yellow flowers. Sometimes we would take our lunches and eat them, sitting on a log. Toward the end of the month, on one such walk we noticed that birds were everywhere.

"Why are there suddenly so many?" asked Debra.

"Maybe because it will soon be nesting time, and they are looking for building sites." Next day I brought a book on birds to read to them and also an old bird feeder I found in the attic. Dan and Toby tied it in a bush by the window where we could watch, and then we filled it with some cracked corn from my father's barn.

"I wish we had some sunflower seeds," I said. "They like that best."

Next day Ellie brought a small bucket full. "My father plants sunflowers along the fence rows, and we feed the seeds to the chickens. He sent you these."

We mixed a handful with the corn, and before the school day ended, a pair of red birds (cardinals) found it. The children were excited and wanted to know if now these birds would stay.

"So long as we feed them, I think they will."

About the same time, Dan discovered a pair of wrens nesting in the eaves above the back door. At play time we would tiptoe around to watch them.

One day Toby went to the water bucket for a drink. The shelf where the bucket sat was by the window where the bird feeder hung. Toby began to wave his arms and put his finger over his lips.

"What is it?" we whispered.

"The red birds! They're building a nest."

We tiptoed over to the window, and he was right. They had chosen the bush just beyond the one where the feeder hung. There a few vines and leaves afforded them a private spot, and they were weaving twigs in and out. By the next day the nest was nearly finished, and we were interested to see that they had lined it with soft grasses and bits of last year's cotton from the surrounding field. By the third day the hen began to lay little speckled, bluish eggs, one every day or two until there were four. We could see them by standing on a bench and looking down into the nest. We kept the window shut and stood in the shadows so as not to frighten the birds.

Now the hen began to set, and we were interested to see what a gallant mate the male was. He would feed the setting hen, and when she needed to leave the nest, he would take her place.

The hen of the wren pair was also setting, and now the loud singing of the two males reverberated through the little schoolroom. When this happened, the children would glance up from their lessons, their eyes shining; they looked beautiful to me.

"Do you know why the males sing like that during nesting time?" I asked them. They didn't know; therefore, I read part of a bird story telling how the males sing to proclaim their territory.

"Pro-pro-claim—what's that?" asked Toby with his usual curiosity.

"It means they are saying to other birds, 'stay away—this is our home.'"

The two bird families hatched simultaneously, and that was another interesting time for the children. We could not see how many fledglings the wrens had because their nest was so deep, but we soon saw that the red birds had hatched three and the parents were kept busy feeding them.

One day Dan was watching the birds when he suddenly became alarmed and ran out the back door. We were preparing for lunch, so we dropped everything and followed to see what the trouble was.

"Toby, bring the ax," he hollered. To the horror of all, Dan had a large snake by the tail, pulling it out of the bush where the red birds nested. When Toby got there with the ax, Dan quickly put an end to the snake.

"I got here j-j-just in time," he panted. It's a chicken snake—a big 'un—he woulda swallowed the little birds an' the mamma too if he coulda got to 'er."

"Dan, you are very brave."

"Oh no'm—I kill 'em all the time. They do away with a lot of our eggs and baby chicks at home."

The parent red birds were flying about, very upset.

"Let's go in and let these birds go back to their nest," I said. "I just hope they will." After a long time we were relieved to see that they did go back.

"I'm sho' glad the eggs are hatched," said Dan. "If settin'

eggs ever get cold, they won't hatch." Dan knew a great deal about all areas of farming. I felt sure that even if he did not finish high school he would be a success. As I thought about that little school in later years, I realized more and more how difficult teaching there would have been for me without Dan's help.

We watched the little birds grow feathers, and of course, in time, they left the nest. Although we still saw them from time to time, we were never again quite so close; but I thought the main result was that the children's philosophy about birds, and maybe other wildlife, had changed. Toby expressed this very well when he said, "I used to have a slingshot. I'd kill the big birds if I could and I'd get the eggs out of the nest." For a moment he hung his head as if in shame—then he looked up with a smile and said, "But I wouldn't do it now."

Dan spoke up and said, "I use my gun to shoot birds, squirrels, and rabbits to get meat fo' the table—b-b-but I really don't like to kill anything."

"Dan, don't feel bad about that. Hunting for food is an old and honorable custom. What's bad is shooting animals or birds just for fun or sport. I had to learn that when I was young."

They all looked at me, and almost in a chorus they said, "But you wouldn't kill things!"

"I did once. My playmate was a little boy who could make slingshots. He made one for me, and we went out to shoot birds. I never thought I would kill one, but I hit a little sparrow and saw it die. I threw the slingshot away and ran home crying. I never wanted to kill anything again."

"W-W-What about snakes?" asked Dan, remembering the one he killed.

"Well, you didn't have much choice there, did you? And

you have to kill them at home to save your chickens. It's very important also to recognize which snakes are poisonous. You see, you'd need to kill a rattler in your yard. You can let a little harmless garter snake go free. Do all of you know which snakes around here are poisonous?"

After a discussion, I was alarmed to see that they did not have this important bit of knowledge. My father had taught me the difference when I was quite young, and I assumed they knew.

"I'll call Miss Bunker and ask her to bring a book on snakes when she comes. In the meantime, look under 'Snakes' in the encyclopedia when you have time."

There was so much yet to teach these children, and now we had only March and part of April left. Could I meet such a challenge?

20

The Magic of Spring

ARCH CAME IN WITH COLD, GUSTY WINDS THAT whistled under the eaves and rattled the time-worn windowpanes. The little saplings that bordered the road were bent to the ground, and the children, having become attached to our two bird families, worried that the young ones, now able to fly about in the low bushes, would be blown away.

"I don't think you need to worry," I comforted them. "It seems that little wild things, like birds, know how to cope with the weather." Still, they could not refrain from peeping out of the windows now and then to see if any were in trouble. In a week or two, the weather took a turn for the better and we felt the first real balminess of spring. The warm spell lasted longer than usual, and under the bright sun there was a sudden burst of bloom on the plum, peach, and pear trees, and each morning the children came with armsful to decorate our room.

It was about this time that we witnessed another of nature's phenomena. Not knowing when Toby's cocoon might hatch, I had asked Dan early in February to take it down from the porch ceiling where it had hung all winter and bring it inside. We then fastened the branch to which the cocoon was attached to our back wall, as far from the heater as possible. Since then we had been so busy that we had almost forgotten about the cocoon when, one day, Toby went back for a drink of water and something caught his attention.

He whirled and ran to me, his eyes as big as silver dollars. "The cocoon," he panted. "Some'n's comin' out. Looks like a bumblebee."

I thought that watching this wonder of nature was worth the interruption, so we put down our studies and followed Toby.

"But I guess it ain't a bee, is it?" he asked, examining the insect more closely.

"I think it is either a moth or a butterfly," I told him. "See those things folded on its back? They must be wings."

It crawled out on the limb, hung upside down, and was very still while the large wings, still very wet, began slowly to unfold. We watched for a while, fascinated, then I said to Toby, "This is going to take a while. Why don't you get your reader [he was now reading fluently at second grade level] and work here while you watch. We'll go on with our lessons and you let us know if anything happens."

We had worked very hard since Christmas, even giving up some of our playtimes, and were nearing the end of our textbooks. The children were as anxious as I to finish them by the time school closed, and they did not complain when we worked overtime.

When we completed our assignments it was lunchtime, but before eating we went back to see what progress the moth or butterfly had made. It was dry enough now for us to determine the color of its wings, which were a delicate yellow-green with pretty designs. I suggested to Minnie that after lunch she paint a picture of it for our walls.

While the children got their lunches, I looked under "moth" in the encyclopedia and found a pretty color plate, showing many varieties. "See children, this is a luna moth, one of the most beautiful." I read them about the four stages of the metamorphose.

"Isn't it strange," said Debra. "So many wonderful things go on around us, and we might never know it."

"We are just lucky," I told them, "that Toby found the cocoon last fall. He had the sharpest eyes and saw what the rest of us didn't."

When we finished lunch and fed scraps to the hound, there was no time to read a chapter in *Tom Sawyer*, the Mark Twain book that we were currently reading, and they were disappointed. "We may have time to read it later," I consoled them.

I thought this was a good time to discuss what to do with the encyclopedias. I called the children up, and they sat around my desk.

"Children, you have enjoyed the encyclopedias so much that Miss Sarah wants you to keep them."

"How'll we do that?" asked Debra. "Divide the books up?"

"No, that would ruin the set. The books must be kept together. What do you think of this? You are three families. There are twelve months in a year. What do you think of each family keeping them four months? When one family has the books, they should make the others welcome to come there and use them if they need to. But never take a book away from the set."

They thought about this for a while and decided it was a good plan.

"Who'll have 'em first?" asked Debra.

"What do you think of beginning with the oldest, who is Dan?" They agreed.

"Then if you'll put them in my car, I'll take them to your house when I leave today; that is, if you'll go along and carry them in."

We then took a few minutes to load the books.

During January and February, there had been so many days when weather prevented our playing outside that we had been able to read all of Louisa May Alcott's *Little Women*, which they loved. Mrs. Tucker asked to borrow any book we had finished, and she was reading that one now. Other ladies in the community had followed her example and came often to borrow books. I was able to bring a few more from home, and both Miss Sarah and Miss Bunker contributed some, so that now we almost had a lending library. I was glad because their community offered no such accommodations. We were putting away our lunch baskets and buckets and feeding the scraps to the hound when Lily exclaimed, "Look! The moth! It's flying!" It looked very lovely as it flitted about the room.

"Children, I have read that moths at this stage seek light, so it will probably go to our windows. Let's put something there for it to light on."

We put vases in the windows holding blossoms the children had brought and in one a fern Mrs. Tucker had given us. Finally, the moth settled on the fern, and there it stayed until school was out. When it was closing time, Dan asked, "Will we shut the moth up in here?"

"Dan, these moths are accustomed to the great out-of-doors. Don't you think it might hurt itself, hitting the walls, and would be safer on the porch?"

"Yes'm—I—I guess so." When Dan moved the fern to the porch, the moth did not attempt to fly.

"It may be laying eggs," I told them.

"Real eggs?" asked Ellie in astonishment, looking at the size of the moth and thinking of the only eggs she knew.

"They will be moth eggs, very tiny; I don't know exactly what they look like, but maybe we'll see some on the fern tomorrow."

As we were preparing to leave, Cammie asked a question that had been on my mind also.

"When can we walk to the woods? I'll bet we could find some'in pretty there now."

"You are right, Cammie. We have almost caught up with our schoolwork, and maybe we could go at noon tomorrow if we start early and finish our assignments by then."

"Could we take our lunches with us and have a picnic?" asked Debra.

"What a nice idea while the weather is so pretty," I responded.

On our return next morning, the moth was gone, but all over the place where it clung to the fern were the eggs it had laid. The children examined them with interest.

"They look like little seeds, don't they?" observed Toby. "Now what will happen to 'em?"

"Why, it's like the article I read to you. In time, they hatch into caterpillars that are tiny at first but they grow and eventually each one will weave a cocoon around itself. The whole cycle is repeated."

The weather was a few degrees warmer, and when it was

time for our walk, we were able to shed our wraps. After the cold winter, the sun felt good on our backs.

The owners of the cotton field were busy plowing under or burning the cotton stalks, getting ready for spring planting. I asked one of the older men what they did about the boll weevil, remembering the stories often told about my father's sad experience.

"Well, we spray as best we kin. But we don't raise cotton the way we done when I wuz a boy."

I would have liked to talk more, but the children were anxious for us to be on our way. To have firm footing, we had to skirt the fields, but there was something interesting to see on every hand. When we reached the woods, there were so many heart leaves popping up that we could hardly avoid stepping on them. We crushed some in our hands so that we could smell the strong scent, which reminded us of ginger.

"D-d-did you ever see the little j-jugs at the roots, Miss Susie?" asked Dan, digging up one with a pointed stick.

"Yes, they hold water for the plant," I was saying when I became interested in something else that came up with the dirt. It had bright colors and wiggled, and I thought it was a caterpillar. Dan took it in his hand, and then I saw what it really was.

"Dan, drop it, quick, and don't touch it again!"

"It's j-jes—a little snake."

"No, it isn't. You'll have to kill it."

"W-why?" he asked, but he crushed the head with his heel. He was puzzled.

"Children," I said with a shiver, "all of you take a good look at that snake. It's the deadly coral snake. Even though it's only a little over a foot long, the venom could kill a person. I've seen only one other, but I've read about them. There is a nonpoisonous snake that is similar to the poison variety. Look closely, and I'll show you some differences. See the bands of red, yellow, and black? On this poisonous kind they go all around the body, see? And the head on this poisonous one is black, whereas the other snake's isn't."

"Dan, carry it carefully, with a stick and we'll put it in a jar of alcohol so you can show it to your families. The venom of this snake is as dangerous as that of the king cobra of India."

It was interesting to see the hound's reaction to the snake. When Dan killed the chicken snake, the hound tried to help, but now he tucked his tail between his legs and kept his distance as if he realized how dangerous this snake could be.

As we walked along, I told the children about the four poisonous snakes in our country. They knew about the cottonmouth moccasin because those were fairly common around creeks, ponds, and similar bodies of water in our area. They had heard of rattlers, but only Dan had seen one. They did not know about the copperhead even though these were common in all of Alabama. I noticed that Lily was shivering and holding on to Minnie.

"It's good to have a dog because they can sense danger and let you know. See, Lily, we don't have to worry because our hound will protect us." Then I changed the subject.

When we reached the creek, the mountain laurel and wild hydrangeas were budding and almost ready to bloom. Dan and Toby climbed along the banks and picked as many as we could carry. The dogwood blooms were still a little green, but we took a few branches, hoping in a week or two to come back and get more.

"Look, Miss Susie, there is a good log over there where we can sit for our picnic," said Dimmie. We found a spot to lay down our greenery, and then we got out our lunches. Birds were singing in every direction.

"Isn't this wonderful, children. The woods are so pretty and the birds are giving us a concert." Little did we know then that this was the last nature walk we would ever have together.

"When we get our schoolhouse all decorated," said Minnie, as she munched on a sandwich, it will look as pretty as it did at our Thanksgiving party. Miss Susie, that was the best time I ever had. I do wish we could have another party."

They all took up the refrain. "Can't we, please, Miss Susie?"

"Well, I have been thinking of something that would be just as good. Have you ever heard of a school 'turnout'?" They did not think they had. "It's a get-together that you have to celebrate the end of school. You put up samples of your work for parents to see as you did at Thanksgiving, and you give a program with songs, readings, and maybe a play; afterward, if the weather is nice, we could have a picnic under the trees and, of course, invite your families and friends to take part in everything."

I thought I had never seen such happy faces—all except Dan's. I allayed his fears by saying, "And Dan, you could be master of ceremonies again." He then gave me one of his nicest smiles.

All the way back to school, we made plans for our school turnout. "But children, you know we'll all have to work doubly hard to finish our textbooks and practice for a program, too," I warned them.

"We would," they all promised, and each child did just that.

21

Miss Bunker Cheers Me Up

W HEN WE GOT BACK, REVEREND MILFORD WAS sitting on the steps waiting for us.

"Howdy, Miss Susie. Howdy, chillun. I see you found somein' purty."

"Yes, sir," I said, shaking his hand, "and we had such a good time."

Dan showed him the snake. (I whispered to Minnie to take Lily inside while we discussed it.)

"This here is one o' them dangerous lil' snakes, ain't it? I've heard tell of 'em but never did see one befo'."

"Dan," I said, "will you see if you can find a jelly glass with a lid? If so, put the snake in it, but be very careful not to touch it, then pour alcohol over it." I kept alcohol for a disinfectant. I sat on the steps beside Reverend Milford.

"Are you just visiting, Reverend Milford, or do you want to see me about something?"

"I ain't got much time, but I jes wanted to tell you we're

holding camp meetin' nex' week an want to invite you an yo' family."

"Oh, thank you. I'll tell my family and we'll try to come, maybe Sunday."

"That'ud be a good day. We bring picnic baskets that day an' have dinner on the ground. It'll be at the reg'lar camp meetin' grounds in Dixons Mills."

"Yes, sir. I went once, but I thought you always held these meetings in summer."

"Yes'm, as a rule we do, but we had the chanc't' to get this good evangelist, Gypsy Smith, an' we couldn't pass that up. He ast me to he'p 'im so I got to go. Got a lot to do. Please invite Miss Sarah and Miss Bunker."

"Good-bye," I said. "We'll try to come, and I'll be sure to invite them."

I watched his stooped shoulders as he went down the road. He had become a good friend, and I hoped I would have the chance to hear him perform from the pulpit.

On the way home with Miss Sarah, I mentioned the camp meeting and gave her Reverend Milford's message.

"I'd love to go, and I do hope I can persuade my parents to go also. They've been shut in all winter, and I think this would do them a world of good. Do you want to go with us?"

"Thank you, Miss Sarah, but if it wouldn't be too much trouble could you take me to Linden on Friday (tomorrow) afternoon? I really need to go home, and I'm hoping my family will go to camp meeting with me Sunday. I'd better call my father as soon as we get to your house."

When I talked to my father, he sounded really happy that I was coming home, and he thought that going to camp meeting was a fine idea. Then, to my request that someone meet me in Linden the next day, he said not to worry, I would surely find someone waiting for me there.

Then I called Miss Bunker and caught her just before she left the office.

"Camp meeting!" she responded with enthusiasm to Reverend Milford's invitation. "I've never been to one, and I've always wanted to go, but I hate to go alone. How about you and your family meeting me in Linden on Sunday morning and going from there in my car? It's larger."

"We'll try, if you'll let us fix the lunch. You'd love my mother's fried chicken."

"Well, that would help, since I board with a family, you know. Now I'm so glad you called because I was going to try to call you. The county board has scheduled the children's examinations for Monday."

"Monday!" I gasped. "B-But Miss Bunker, that's too soon. We-we're not ready! We haven't quite finished our textbooks!"

"Susie, that really doesn't matter in exams like those. I'm familiar with them; they just test the children's general information according to ages and grades. There is nothing to worry about."

"Oh, but Miss Bunker, there is. I'm scared, really scared. They might not pass!"

"Honey, why are you scared of that?" she asked kindly.

Then I blurted out all the fears that must have been building up inside me ever since I knew there would be county examinations.

"Miss Bunker, when I accepted the school, I was so young and thoughtless and was thinking only of myself. I didn't know anything about teaching; you know that. If I had not accepted the job, maybe those children could have had the experienced teacher they deserved."

"Susie, I'm ashamed of you."

"Ashamed?" By now I could not hold back the tears.

"Yes, ashamed! In one light what you say makes sense, but knowing what I know about that school, about those children, and about you, what you say is not the real truth at all."

"What is, Miss Bunker? Please tell me, I need to know."

"Well, as I see it, neither you nor the people who hired you had any choice but to do what you both did. They had tried experienced teachers and they did not work out. Anyway, experienced teachers can demand better than your school can offer. But you—you were glad to get the job, and it was your only chance to continue college and, child, I want to say this, and I mean it, even the angels in heaven could not have tried any harder than you have. You have succeeded! Not only have you taught those children a great deal, but you've given them love and an appreciation of their world."

"You really think so, Miss Bunker?"

"I wouldn't say it if I didn't. You are right about one thing. You knew nothing of teaching. If you'll excuse the expression, you didn't know a damned thing. At first, you couldn't have done it without me, but you learned. I want to tell you that working with you and your little school was the most fun and the most rewarding thing I ever experienced." There was a long pause, then she said, "And now, why do you want to throw it all away?"

"Throw it away, Miss Bunker?"

"Yes, that's what you'll do if you don't get hold of yourself. I really think those children have a chance to do quite well on the exams. I'm not sure, but I think so, that is, provided you are behind them. If you're scared, they'll be too. You must have confidence in yourself and in them. That is going to be the most important of all. I've worked with children a long time, and I know."

By this time, I was feeling thoroughly ashamed.

"Miss Bunker, I'll do better! I promise!"

"Now I must tell you something the superintendent said that should make you feel better."

"Please tell me," I said, needing some good news.

"He said that anytime in the future when you need a teaching job, you may always be assured of one in Marengo County as long as he is superintendent."

"Oh, how nice. Tell him I thank him."

"Now get a good night's sleep and don't worry. You've got to tell those children about the exams tomorrow and how you do it will be crucial to them. You've got to be honest with them, of course, but I think you have good reason to be encouraging. Just remember that making them feel you believe in them will do more good than any bits of knowledge that you might wish to cram them with at the last minute. Now I hope we can get together Sunday, not to talk shop, but to have a good time; just let me know. Good-bye, and remember what I said."

Remember! How could I ever forget! Miss Bunker had gotten me through many rough spots during my teaching year, and I believed in her completely, but now I felt the need to be alone and come to grips with myself. I could hear Miss Sarah discussing the camp meeting with her parents so I let myself out the front door and closed it softly behind me.

The night air had all the chilliness of an early spring twilight, but I was hardly aware of it. As I walked down the worn path toward the road, my mind went back to that August afternoon when I took the teaching contract out of Mr. Dick's hand and signed it with so much enthusiasm. Had I thought at all about the pupils I would teach? No, I hadn't. I doubt if I could have because they hardly existed in my mind then. They were just eight young people without faces or personalities; they became real only when I met them on our first day of school. But I was sure that from that moment on there was good chemistry between us out of which grew the mutual love and faith in each other so I did not feel at fault there.

Then how did the deep guilt feeling arise? I was sure it was because I feared the terrible possibility that I had not taught the children enough to enable them to pass the exams; but if I had to do it over, with all the problems I faced, could I have done any better or any differently? I did not think so.

I sat down on a stump beside the path where Miss Sarah and I sometimes sat to watch the sunsets, and I pondered the question for a long time. I knew that I could not remember a time in my life when I had tried so hard to succeed at anything as I had in that little school. So I felt that the answer had to be "No! I could not have done differently." Then I realized that that was what Miss Bunker was trying to tell me. As always when I followed her advice or philosophy, burdens fell from my shoulders as a heavy harness did from a mule's back at the end of a hard day. I was filled again with the optimism that was a part of my nature, and I knew I could face (with the children) whatever lay ahead. Just then I heard Miss Sarah ringing the bell for supper, and I hurried back up the path with a lighter heart.

22

We Go to Camp Meeting

I AWOKE NEXT MORNING TO A WORLD THAT SEEMED more beautiful to me than usual. I sang at my bath, and I sang as I packed to go home. I was still singing when I went down the hall to breakfast.

"You surely sound happy this morning," observed Miss Sarah as we sat down together at the table. She pushed a plate of golden biscuits over to me. "Butter some while they're hot."

I broke open a couple and put fresh butter between; then I poured out my story to her.

"I don't know. Maybe I don't have anything to sing about, but at least I've faced a problem and feel ready to deal with it."

Miss Sarah looked at me and waited, holding a knife with butter on it in midair.

"You see," I explained, "the children are scheduled to have county examinations in Linden on Monday. I have to tell them this morning."

"So?" she asked, still not seeing my problem.

"Well, when Miss Bunker first told me this news last night,

I was scared to death that the children might not pass, and I would feel responsible. I almost went to pieces."

"How does Miss Bunker feel about the situation?"

"Why, she is optimistic about what the children can do, but she says that my own feelings will affect them."

"Don't you think she is right?"

"I do now, and I think I'm ready to face whatever happens."

"Good! I'm glad." She passed the platter of eggs and sausages. "Eat your breakfast now and enjoy it."

When Miss Sarah and I rode through the pasture, the patches of fog in the low places had not quite lifted, and the mist hung over the road by the school like a soft wedding veil. Yet I could dimly see the children waiting for me on the porch as always. In years to come, when I thought of those dear children and the little schoolhouse, the picture that came most often to my mind was of them waiting and watching for me there regardless of the weather, just as they were doing now. When we reached the gap, Dan had it open.

"I'll be here at three to take you to Linden. Have a good day," called Miss Sarah as she rode away.

Whether we had a good day, I thought, depended largely on how the children took the news of the exams. I felt ready to tell them but had decided to try not to make too much of it.

"Children," I said as soon as we were settled, "there is something we need to discuss before we begin our work." They came and stood around my desk. "Remember, I told you we would have county examinations in Linden?"

"Yes'm," said Minnie, "but since Cluster and me are gettin' married, I don't have to take 'em, do I?"

"We'll discuss that in a few minutes, Minnie. I talked to Miss Bunker by phone last night and she said the examinations are scheduled for Monday morning."

The children were always waiting at the little schoolhouse.

"So soon!" exclaimed Debra, "but we haven't quite finished all of our textbooks."

"I told her that, Debra, and she said that would not matter for the type of exams we'll take."

"Now, Minnie, about your taking them, I don't suppose you are compelled to do so, but later you might wish you had because many people continue school after they marry—even after they have families."

"Suppose I don't pass?"

"Oh, well, that's something we all face. So what if you don't pass? There's nothing lost in trying."

"I-I-I'm gonna try," said Dan. "An' Minnie, I'll be mo' likely to fail than you. I've missed so much of school." Minnie did not respond. She sat deep in thought.

"How'll we all get there?" asked Cammie, serious for once.

"I'll take my car and Miss Bunker has told me several times that we can count on hers. She suggests that everyone bring a sandwich—nothing more because she has a surprise for us. Now I must tell you this: Miss Bunker thinks that because of the good work you've done in school, you should do well, and I think so too!" I could hear sighs of relief.

"What are these 'xam's like?" asked Toby.

"Toby, I don't know. But Miss Bunker knows, and she says we shouldn't worry. When the exams are over, maybe we'll have fun that day. Now, before we get down to work, I'd like to know if you are all going to the camp meeting this Sunday."

"Cluster is going to take our family," said Minnie, her face beaming happily. "Pa has already gone down there."

"We're goin'," said Ellie, "and we're gonna take Dan an' Debra."

"I'm so glad all of you will be there because I'm hoping my family will go, and I want you to meet each other." They seemed happy at the prospect, and I was glad we had it to take our minds off the exams. Then we got down to work and nothing further interrupted our usual routine.

On the way to Linden that afternoon, Miss Sarah and I talked about what to wear, what would be appropriate to take for "dinner-on-the-ground," whether we could sit together, and things of that nature. Then she brought up a subject that we had avoided but one that had been on our minds—her wedding.

"We are going to have a very simple home wedding in June. I don't have any near relatives, you know, so Miss Susie, will you stand up for me, be my maid of honor?" asked Sarah.

"Of course I will. I only hope I can find something appropriate to wear."

"We are not going to dress fancy."

"I know my mother will help me," I said. "She sews beautifully." And so it was settled. I wondered what would happen to Miss Sarah's parents, left alone, but I did not ask. As things turned out, I never got to see the wedding, but we did not know that then.

On Sunday we joined Miss Bunker in Linden and went with her to the camp meeting as she had requested. I was proud of our lunch: potato salad, fried chicken, homemade rolls, and pound cake. We had a gallon jug of lemonade, and we were told that ice would be available at the campgrounds.

During that time, the road we traveled to Dixons Mills was narrow and winding, often among scrub pines and dense foliage, with very few dwellings in sight. I wondered where all the people lived who attended these meetings. When we reached the village, we soon learned where the campgrounds were because we came upon a sign pointing the direction, and already there was a long line of vehicles heading that way. We fell in line and followed them.

After we had gone a short distance, the foliage and trees thinned away and we came to a wide open area which was the entrance to the much publicized Dixons Mills Campgrounds, known far and wide for its size and fine religious programs. Located on a crossroads and near the entrance was the huge pavilion whose seating area was as large as or larger than that of any church I had ever attended. It had a shingled roof and rough floor on which were numerous homemade benches that were rapidly being filled with the visitors. At the far end was a platform, which I assumed served as the pulpit. Reverend Milford sat talking to a dark, handsome young man who, no doubt, was the evangelist Gypsy Smith. Nearby a lady was playing soft hymnal music on a small portable organ. Behind the pavilion were many cabins, plank tables, pits for cooking, and other buildings as far as I could see.

A lady standing nearby, who was one of the many hostesses,

said to me, "Want me to show you around?" She seemed anxious to oblige.

"I'd like that."

"Surprised at the size of this place?" she asked, watching my expression as I looked at the many buildings.

"Surprised!" I exclaimed. "I've heard about it but never dreamed it was so large. How did it all come about, way out here in the woods?"

"Well, a few men and women had a dream, inspired by God, you might say. It's a long story and if I told you all, we'd miss the service. The first meeting was held in 1911 or 1912 and by 1913 it was well organized and incorporated. People came from all over the country to contribute and help with the building. In the beginning there were over a hundred cabins and all the other things you see here."

When we got to the pavilion, people were still coming in wagons, surreys, and buggies, some walking or on horseback. There were a good many cars, mostly Model T's, and many of them had out-of-state tags. There were even a few very old covered wagons that seemed to be filled with camping equipment.

Reverend Milford was standing and waiting for all to be seated and to get quiet. He held up his hand, and a hush fell over the congregation. "Friends," he said, "we are very fortunate to have with us today one of the great evangelists of our time, the Reverend Gypsy Smith."

The tall, handsome young man stood and bowed and gave the crowd a heartwarming smile. Then he sat down and Reverend Milford continued. I had been told that Reverend Milford had a beautiful speaking voice, and it was true. I'm sure he made the usual grammatical errors, but they were hardly noticeable, and I could understand how he could deliver a spellbinding sermon. He read an appropriate Scripture, followed by a prayer, then he turned to the choir: "Be nice did y'all lead us in that ol' favorite, 'Blest Be the Tie That Binds.'"

Something about the quality of the song touched me way down deep, and for a moment I felt as though I were back in the church of my childhood. Then I saw the reason. They had invited my father to join the choir. His rich bass voice reached me when no other could, and this dear familiar hymn made my day.

Just as the song was finished, another group of people walked up. This puzzled me until Reverend Milford said, "You mus' be the folks who rode the loggin' train. Come in an' welcome!" Without being asked, the young people and children gave up their seats to the visitors. One of the hostesses had brought quilts so that in the end no one had to sit on the bare ground.

Now Reverend Milford retired to the back because the moment had arrived for which the big gathering had been waiting: the sermon by the great Gypsy Smith. I have never heard another who kept the congregation spellbound as did this great evangelist. When he came forward, an open Bible in his hand, and began to speak, every man, woman, and child seemed to fall into a trance that lasted throughout the entire sermon.

When the services were over, I heard a familiar voice call my name. It was Reverend Milford. He wanted to introduce me to the Reverend Gypsy Smith.

"Gypsy, this here is Miss Susie, our schoolteacher. We're mighty proud o' her."

The evangelist gave me a thrill by shaking my hand and saying, "Yours is a noble profession. I aspired to be a teacher once."

"You certainly chose the right one as minister," I said. "I enjoyed your message so much. I enjoyed hearing you, too, Reverend Milford. We have had a wonderful meeting."

"I met your father, and we had a nice talk," said Reverend Milford.

"I wish you could meet my mother, too. You'd love her."

"I hope I can, but we got a lotta folks to see." They said good-bye and were gone. I turned to the children. "You can meet my mother, can't you?"

"Effen we hurry," said Minnie. "We have to help my mother fix the table because the Reverend Smith is gonna eat with us."

Dan and Toby were standing close by so I beckoned to them to come, too. We found my mother, Miss Bunker, and Miss Sarah, busy like all the ladies there, fixing for what they called "dinner-on-the-ground." Actually, we ate on the long plank tables.

The children loved my mother, as I knew they would. She knew each one from my description of them.

"Where is Elizabeth? I want my pupils to meet her, too."

"Some of her Linden classmates have invited her to eat with them," my mother said, "and Daddy is eating at a special table for the choir."

The midday sun was almost as warm as in summer, and we were thankful for the shade of a spreading oak tree. When the meal was finally over, we collected our family for the trip back to Linden.

"What did Reverend Milford mean about those folks coming on a logging train?" asked Miss Bunker when we were on our way.

"I can explain that," I told her. "You see, many people in that area are in the lumber business because of the vast acreage of pine forests around there. Different lumber companies built small rail lines with real little steam engines for hauling out logs. Some of these carry passenger cars for people who want to travel on them. They are very crude cars, open to the elements and with only long benches to sit on. When my Aunt Frances taught in Dixons Mills, there were very few roads in the area and she got there by riding this logging train. Her description of that trip is amusing. She said many of the passengers that day were carrying butter, eggs, chickens, and the like, and the conductor, who knew everybody, would stop every so often for them to deliver their wares. When he took up my aunt's ticket, he said to her, 'You're Miss Frances, the new schoolteacher, ain't you?' She told him she was and asked how he knew. He said he knew everybody else on the train so she had to be the new teacher.

"When they were approaching Dixons Mills, the conductor asked her, 'Miss Frances, you want to get off at the crossing or the gen'ral store?' She said no one had told her where to get off so he said, 'Well, don't worry. Mr. Dixon is gonna meet you. I'll stop at the crossing an' if he ain't there, then he'll be at the gen'ral store,' and the store it was, according to my aunt."

"I understand," said Miss Bunker, "that there used to be many camp meeting grounds, but that there are very few left." We were glad that we had had the opportunity to attend one that was such an important part of a respected and old tradition. (The Dixons Mills camp meetings were discontinued in 1936 because of polio epidemics.)

In Linden we lifted the sleeping Wee into our own car, and Miss Bunker bade us good-bye. "The exams are scheduled for 10:00 so I'll see you at school about 8:30," she said with a smile, and drove away.

Next morning at school, I found the children waiting, as

usual. They were dressed in their best, and each carried a sandwich. I thought they seemed relaxed and happy, even Minnie, who ran out to meet me.

"Miss Susie, I'm gonna take the tests as you wish. Ma and Pa agree with you that it would be best for me to do it, an' I'm willin'."

"I'm so glad, Minnie. I see Miss Bunker coming. Now four of you ride with her and four with me."

When we reached the building of the County Board, we found that a place was prepared for each grade and a teacher was waiting with the necessary tests. Children from other sections were there for the same purpose as our children, and this seemed to make ours feel better.

The tests for the older children lasted about two hours. I sat in the hall most of the time and waited while Miss Bunker went from room to room, giving help. The first of our children to finish was Toby. He came out beaming.

"Wasn't hard a bit," he said. "I jus' had to do a lotta readin' an' 'rithmetic. I'm so thirsty."

I took him down the hall to a water fountain. When we returned, all of the girls were waiting, and last was Dan. The girls agreed with Toby that the tests were not hard, but Dan seemed tired.

"'Twas hard for me," he said, "but I done it." Toby led them down the hall to the drinking fountain while I waited anxiously for Miss Bunker, hoping she would have the test results soon. When she finally came, I was almost afraid to ask; then she smiled broadly, and somehow I knew the news was good.

"Not only did they all pass, but the teachers think Toby should be promoted to third grade."

"Third grade!"

"Yes. He passed the second grade tests with flying colors."

I was so relieved that I sat down and leaned my head back against the wall. Yes, it was a beautiful day, just as I had thought.

"Now it's time to have some fun," said Miss Bunker with a smile. "I know a drugstore that has an ice cream parlor in the back with tables and chairs. I want to treat everyone to drinks to go with the sandwiches and then ice cream.

"And," I added, "my mother sent a box of tea cakes to help out." I could hardly wait to see the faces of the children when they heard all the good news.

23

Planning the Last Two Weeks of School

THE MONTH WAS APRIL, AND I WAS DRIVING DOWN the same little road in Marengo County, Alabama, over which I had traveled in September, when this story began. That September morning seemed so long ago, yet only seven months had passed and some things had not changed. I was wearing the same dress as before, more worn and faded from wear and washing, but I was saving every penny I made for college and buying new clothes was out of the question. I was driving the same little Model T Ford, and again I would cut off the motor at the top of each hill and coast to save gasoline.

I was as happy as I had been on that first morning and sang as I rode along, but somehow there was a difference. My happiness was now tinged with a bit of sadness over the parting soon to take place between the children and me and with other good friends such as Miss Bunker and Miss Sarah and her family. There was an even greater difference in me, which I could not put into words. It had something to do with maturity, I think, but a maturity that came with a price. I was leaving behind in that little one-room school a part of my girlish fervor and youth, but it had all been worth it.

There were two more weeks of school, and we had much to do. That day in Linden, when we had finished our exams and had eaten lunch, the children asked if they might walk around and see the window displays in stores. Their families were busy and seldom visited the neighboring towns, and we thought it a good idea; besides, it gave Miss Bunker and me time for a private conversation about how we would spend the rest of the school year.

"Take your time and have fun," said Miss Bunker, waving the children off.

But Dan still lingered, shuffling from one foot to the other. Finally, he got out what he wanted to say.

"M-M-Miss Bunker, I-I've saved some of my school money which I was paid fo b-buildin' the fires. I wanta buy somein' fo' my fam'ly. A sh-shirt fo' Pa an' dress goods fo' Ma an' Debra. C-could you tell me the bes' sto's?"

"What a nice idea, Dan. I'll write the names of two down for you." She wrote and handed him the slip. "One store is at the end of this block, the other, across the street and down a block." He hurried off to join the others and do his shopping.

"Now let's talk about school," she said. "Are you planning a turnout as you mentioned to me once?"

"Oh, yes! The children are enthusiastic and are already learning their parts. We have some wonderful surprises so promise me you'll be there."

"I'll do my best to make it."

"You've got to do better than that. You *must* be there because things are going to come alive that day in that little school in the cotton patch."

"All right," she said, laughing. "I'll be there, the Lord being willing. Now, besides the program, what are your plans for the rest of the time?"

"I was going to ask you, but I thought we'd spend half the day finishing our textbooks and the other half practicing, unless you have a better idea."

"Oh, that sounds fine. I think giving that program will be a fine learning experience, especially for children as isolated as these. By the way, the state school supervisor will be in Linden for a few days. She wants to visit our school."

"Oh, goodness! What for?"

"Because I've told her about it, and she wants to meet you and to see the school."

"Oh, dear! I hope she'll like what she sees."

"I know she will so don't you start worrying. I'll call and tell you what day to expect us. Will you please do something for me? Let her see you give a spelling lesson."

Of course, I would do anything for Miss Bunker. I remembered the day she arrived just as we began spelling and how she had laughed. This was early in the school year. We always faced the problem of getting through so many grades in one day. I combined as many as I could, and then I had what I thought was a bright idea about the spelling. The children were all at different levels, but I saw no reason why I could not hear all grades at the same time.

"Boys and girls, you know what a time we have finishing all of our lessons by three o'clock. Yesterday we did not get to spelling so I want us to try something different tomorrow."

"May I try, too?" asked Toby.

"I don't see why not, but you are all going to have to study your spelling so well that you know which are your words.

Then you won't get mixed up when I call the next person." I wrote Toby six two-letter words, but he seemed disappointed.

"I already know how to spell these," he said. I threw the paper in the wastebasket and wrote three-letter words. "Will these do?" I asked.

"I-I guess so, but I know some of these, too."

Next day I tried out my plan. I would point to Toby, call his word, then do the same with Lily, and likewise up through all the grades, then start over and quickly do the same with their next words. Cammie got mixed up once. After I helped her, we had no more trouble. As time went on, the children became more and more adept at following this plan in the spelling. One day we had just started a lesson when Miss Bunker arrived. She waved to me to go on with what we were doing while she sat and watched from a back seat. As we were about to finish, I glanced up to see Miss Bunker with her handkerchief over her mouth to muffle any sound but with every inch of her large, voluptuous frame shaking with laughter. I took up the papers, glancing at each to be sure it had a name and date.

"You may have a short recess while I talk to Miss Bunker," I told the children. After speaking to Miss Bunker, they hurried out, happy over the unexpected playtime. Now, with them gone, Miss Bunker joined me, openly laughing and wiping her eyes.

"That was the fastest spelling lesson I ever saw," she said.

"I have to do these things, else I'd never get through all the grades," I told her seriously.

"Oh, honey, I didn't mean to sound critical," she said. "Oh, no, I made a mental note of your method so I can pass it on to some other struggling young teacher. Let's look at each paper and see how the children did."

We sat down together, and each took about half of the pa-pers.

"We might as well grade them as we go and save you the trouble," she said.

As we would have guessed, Toby and Debra had perfect papers and so did Tammy. Lily and Ellie each missed one word. None of the others missed more than two.

Miss Bunker smiled. "I think they did very, very well."

"Thank you—I'll tell them you said so."

When Miss Bunker said good-bye that day, she reminded me that she would let me know what day to expect her and the state supervisor. I could only groan!

As I was about to leave our home for school on Friday morning, our neighbor, Mr. Edward Eppes, met me at the gate.

"I'm glad I caught you," he said. "I have good news. James Masengill got home late last night."

"He did! I had a letter saying he was coming for a short visit, but he did not know what day."

"I have a great idea. You know how James loves fishing. What do you say we surprise him with a fish fry this evening on Bogue Creek? The weather is perfect for it."

"That would be great, but as you see, I have no time to help, Mr. Edward."

"You don't need to. I'll tell James and ask all the ladies to make sandwiches in case we catch no fish. You get out at three?"

I nodded. "Then wait for us at your school and I'll drop James by; he can drive your car, and your school is not so far from Bogue Creek. I'll attend to everything."

"I do wish I could do something, but I have to go. Can I drop you off anywhere?"

"No, I'll go in and tell your mother about the fish fry. See you this afternoon. Since you'll have the family car, I'll take your folks to the Bogue."

"Thank you, Mr. Edward. Good-bye."

When I got to the store, Elizabeth was still there, waiting for the bus. I told her about the fish fry, and she thought it would be fun, but Daddy said he and Mr. Gene had to work on the books. "But I'll be home in time to help Rosa with Wee so Mamma can go."

While we were talking, the phone rang. It was Miss Bunker calling me.

"Susie, I apologize for being so late telling you this, but I just found out. The state supervisor just came by, and we are coming to visit your school this afternoon. See you there and don't worry."

I nearly dropped in my tracks. How could I not worry! I needed to get to school and get things ready. I told Daddy and Elizabeth good-bye and drove away, going a little faster than usual. I had planned to stop by the Masengill home to speak to James, but now I did not have time.

James was the Masengills' son nearest my age and a dear friend who for many years had escorted me to parties and accompanied me on horseback rides and other outings. It was a standing joke that when I went off to school, if the village teacher was young and attractive, James would fall in love with her. His sister, also my good friend, would write me about it saying, "I'm afraid you've lost James."

But when I came home for vacation and the old steam-drawn train engine puffed into the station at Gallion, James was there as usual to meet me. James had a cute sense of humor, and I could not refrain from teasing him, asking where he'd hidden the teacher. These episodes almost always ended by James telling me all about his love affairs and in turn I would tell him about any romantic episodes I had had while I was away. Once over, they were always funny. James was very romantic, and he had many, but through the years our friendship survived them all.

I had not seen him for about six months because he had been working in southeastern Florida. He would be home only a few days before joining his sisters in Pittsburgh, where another job awaited him. Of course, we had no way of foreseeing the future; James would marry in Pittsburgh and live there the rest of his life.

As I rode toward my school, I couldn't help thinking how much I would have to look forward to if only there was no state supervisor to worry about. I finally came to the conclusion that all I could do was run the school as usual and hope for the best.

24

The State Supervisor
Visits My School

BOUT ONE O'CLOCK, JUST AS WE WERE COMING IN
from play, Miss Bunker and her friend drove into the
yard. The children, who had grown very fond of
Miss Bunker, quickly surrounded her car. Dan
gallantly opened the car door for her while Toby reached for
her arm to assist her in getting out.

"Susie, and boys and girls, I want you to meet Mrs. Taylor."
Then she introduced each child by name. Though the two
women were opposites in appearance, Mrs. Taylor tall and
thin and Miss Bunker short and plump, they had one striking
resemblance. When they communicated with children, their
eyes radiated a certain softness, and the children responded in
turn.

Before beginning the spelling exercise, we took the women
on a tour of our schoolroom.

With Toby leading the way, we took them from front to
back. The expression on Miss Bunker's face was one of pride,
but I could not fathom that on the face of our visitor. When

she did express herself, it was very revealing. "I've visited schools all over Alabama from the mountains to the Gulf," she said. "I've been to mining camps, to remote country places—oh, more than I can count—but I've never seen one quite like this."

"What do you mean?" I asked.

"I've seen buildings as crude as this, some, but not many, but what you've done with it is amazing." She walked around pointing out what she liked: "The pictures and all the good work on the walls, flowers, foliage, and all the things that make us one with nature; a rough, hand-built bookcase with a set of encyclopedia so old that most people would throw it away. I can see they are used here. There is the shell of a cocoon where a butterfly or moth must have hatched. Everywhere I look, there is something. A flag, a map, why, the knowledge and beauty that radiate from these walls make this room a lovely and inspiring place to be. Miss Susie, did you or the children do all this?"

"Oh, the children did most of it, they really did."

"Yes, that is as it should be, but don't ever forget, you were the inspiration." She said this with such a loving smile that I was truly glad she had come, and I said so.

"I knew you'd be," said Miss Bunker. "Now it's late so we'd better have that spelling lesson."

The two ladies sat down on a back seat while the children sat in a semicircle with their paper and pencils. I was so intent on making the lesson a good one that I failed to hear a car door slam, and before I realized it, Mr. Edward and James were coming in the door. The way the door opened, it hid our visitors from their view, and although I could see that the men were playing a cute joke, I froze with embarrassment and could not speak. They had rolled up James's pants and put a little boy's hat on his head. He had his finger in his mouth like a timid little boy on his first day of school, and Mr. Edward was leading him by the hand.

"Susie," Mr. Edward said, "here's a new pupil and he knows the first lesson" (that lesson being that he loves his teacher).

I did not laugh; I did not even smile. My eyes were riveted on the two women, who sat behind the door. The men dropped the pose and, following my gaze, they turned quickly and saw the visitors. It was their turn to look horror-struck.

"Oh, ma'am we're so sorry; we didn't know."

It was the first time I had ever seen Mr. Edward at a loss for words. Both women were laughing, and Miss Bunker saved the day.

"That was a cute joke," she said, shaking hands with the men and introducing themselves. James, who had a good sense of humor, was the first to recover. I breathed a sigh of relief and joined them, and soon we were all laughing, especially at James's funny getup.

"That spelling lesson was amazing," said Mrs. Taylor. I never saw one go so fast," and she laughed at that too.

Finally, Mr. Edward was on his way while James sat in my car and waited for me to finish the school day. It turned out beautifully, including a wonderful fish fry on Bogue Creek. I did not completely regain my composure until after Mr. Edward caught an eel and tied it on a long string, which he then fastened to my belt. He then yelled, "Snake!"

The eel, resembling a black snake, seemed to be after me. I grabbed Mr. Edward, and for the second time that day his joke backfired. I somehow tangled the string around his legs, making the eel appear to climb up his back. We all had such a good laugh that finally I was able to shake off any tension I had left from the two frightening experiences. I whacked my tormentor good across the rear with a stick and then as we watched the April sun set behind the trees, we lolled in the warmth of the dying embers and sang old songs until the moon took over. James's arm around my shoulders felt good in the chill of the spring twilight so I forgot all the problems of school and let the romance of the evening take over as we listened to James's stories of his adventures in the Florida Everglades.

25

The School Turnout

THE DAY FOR OUR SCHOOL TURNOUT DAWNED AS bright and balmy as any April day that I could remember. The children and I had given this program our best, and I didn't think I was being too boastful when I spread the word that this turnout was something people should not miss.

The afternoon before, the children's fathers helped us fix the seating as usual and stretched a wire to mark the stage. Then, with sheets dangling on safety pins for curtains, everything was ready. Dan practiced pulling them over and over. Cammie clasped her hands and whispered, "Like a real stage, ain't, aren't it."

The program consisted of many readings and skits, all enclosed within the plot of a play entitled *Johnny and the Queen*. We had kept two secrets concerning the program, but it was certainly no secret who would play the part of Johnnie. Of course, it was Toby, and I suppose he had a right to strut and brag because, after all, he was the star of the show. Everyone tried to guess who would play the Queen, but so far, no one had the correct answer. Who would play the part of the cross old gatekeeper was also a deep dark secret.

It was the last day of the school, and the play was scheduled for two o'clock. By one-thirty, parents and friends filled every seat, and children filled each space on the floor. I knew these people arrived early for any event, and I had prepared something to fill in the gap. I had studied dramatics in college, and my teacher complimented my interpretation of Mark Twain's *Tom Sawyer* whitewashing the fence for his Aunt Polly. I had brushed up on it and surprised the people by coming outside the curtain and saying, "I apologize for putting myself on the program, but since you have thirty minutes to wait, I think you'll have to put up with me." I explained a little about the story and the character and plunged into it, not knowing whether they would like it.

At first, there was a look of curiosity on their faces, then they began to comprehend and to laugh. They even laughed in the wrong places, but it finally went over.

It was soon time for the play, and Dan, dressed in his best, came out and announced the characters. He and I pulled the curtains, and there was Toby. He walked around, talking.

"I surely do want to go to this fair because I hear the Queen will be there. I wonder what I have to do to get in." He wandered over to the other side of the stage, where the fathers had made us a gate with "Fair" painted above it. A bell hung there, and Toby rang it. The gatekeeper appeared and, wonder of wonders, the part was played by Dan and Debra's father, Mr. Tucker, who was a born comedian. He had dressed for the part, and that brought down the house. The men clapped, they whistled, and some stood up. Finally, they got quiet so the play could proceed. Mr. Tucker made up his own words most of the time, and they were funnier than the actual script.

"Boy, what do you want?" he asked Toby.

"What do you have to do to go to this fair?"

"Well, the Queen will be there and you have to do something or give something for her. What you got?"

Toby pulled out his pockets.

"You see I got no money?"

"Well, can you perform?"

"What's that?"

"Sing or say a poem, dance or some'n'." Toby shook his head.

"Then go away boy, and leave me alone."

Toby came back where he had started and sat down, looking very disconsolate.

Lily, Cammie, Ellie, and Tammy came along. They each had a chair; they came to the center of the stage and sat as if around a table and gave a skit, partly in pantomime, about four ladies sipping tea and gossiping about their neighbors. To make it funnier, some of the names were the actual ones of parents and neighbors. This brought much laughter. When they finished and went to the gate, the keeper was there, and he complimented their performance.

"Wait!" called Toby, running over to them. "Can't I go with you?" They drew themselves up haughtily and walked off without him. The gatekeeper picked up a stick and shook it at Toby, saying, "Boy, I tol' you now, git goin'." Toby went back and sat down, his head on his knees.

Debra and Minnie then came in, Debra dressed as a country boy and Minnie as a country girl. They gave a reading called "Sparking Peggy Jane," which was very funny and appealed to the crowd.

The program progressed in the same fashion with the girls giving various skits and readings and with Toby, who wanted so much to see the Queen, becoming such a nuisance to the gatekeeper that the old man finally chased him all the way across the stage with a stick.

Toby now was so tired that he laid down and went to sleep. At that instant, a beautiful lady, all dressed in white, came out on her way to the fair. People did not know who she was at first, then I could hear whispers of "Miss Sarah." "Can that be Miss Sarah?" Yes, it truly was! She was our biggest surprise. She pretended not to know her way so she shook Toby and said, "Little boy! Can you help me? I'm looking for the fair and I've lost my way."

Toby rubbed his eyes and jumped up.

"I can help you, ma'am." He took her arm and guided her across the stage to the gate. The gatekeeper, sitting with his back to the fence, was nodding. Toby shook him, and when the old man opened his eyes, he was about to chase Toby again when he saw the pretty lady.

"Excuse me, ma'am. Can I help you?"

"Yes. I'd like to go to the fair, and I'm taking this little boy with me."

"But ma'am, he caint," the gatekeeper started to say, but before he could, the lady reached in her bag and pulled out a golden crown which she put on her head. The gatekeeper gasped with shocked surprise, then he bowed low.

"Your Majesty!" he said.

"Your Majesty!" said Toby, doing the same.

"Come, little boy. Will you escort me to the fair?"

Toby stood as tall as he could and held out his arm to the Queen. They then passed through the gate to the fair. And that was the end of the play.

Dan and I closed the curtains momentarily. When we opened them again, Miss Sarah came out holding hands with all the children. Finally, even Dan joined them, and they sang "God Bless America."

Last of all I stood and bade farewell to a bunch of country people for whom I had grown to have great love and respect. The children and I had agreed not to say good-bye because we felt sure we would see each other now and then, but time and circumstances can alter the best of intentions and I never saw some of those children again. I have thought of them often, and I'm sure they have of me. As I write about them now, sixty-five years later, I relive clearly, in my dreams, the events of the year taught in that little one-room school.

Epilogue

WHEN THE FINAL PAGES OF MY BOOK WERE written, some questions were still unanswered, such as, What happened to the children? What about your education? Did you go back to Montevallo long enough to get your degree?

I could most easily answer those questions concerning myself. Yes, by going three summers and taking an extra load in the winters, I was able to graduate with my class. This seemed very important to me at the time, because I had many friends in that group.

My financial problems were solved by money I saved from teaching and by three scholarships. When more money was needed, I again painted coats-of-arms for faculty friends, and for one I copied paintings of old masters. It was not easy, but there always seemed to be a way to solve financial difficulties.

I eventually married and raised two children of my own, both of whom received university degrees and went on to follow wherever their work led, sometimes to far-off places.

Learning about the children I taught was much more difficult. I located an older sister of one of the children I taught
and we talked quite a while long-distance. Some of the families had moved farther south and we had moved to Tuscaloosa,
making the distance between us greater. I did find that Ellie
lives out on a route from Greensboro which is only about sixty
miles away. My husband died a few years ago and my children
live far away, but I hope to go with friends some Sunday afternoon to see Ellie in person if we can find her.

I have learned that the Tuckers are still running a small
dairy below Linden. I went to see them a few years ago and
luckily both Dan and Debra were home. Their sister, a nurse,
had gotten Debra into nursing school and she was doing fine.
Dan had to do all the running of the dairy because of his
father's ill health. But he was happily married and had a pretty
rosy-cheeked baby of whom he was very proud. Dan did not
get to finish high school although he wanted to badly. I understood his problem.

When I visited Old Spring Hill a few years ago, I found that
the Douglas family was still living in the same place, and I
went to see them. Ellie met me at the door, as I had told her I
would come. She was tall and still very pretty. It was a happy
reunion. She was married but had no children. Then the
mother told me some sad and shocking news about Toby. He
was in an auto accident and killed. That was a pity because he
had finished high school, had gotten a job, and was saving all
the money he earned to attend a nearby junior college and
finish his education.

I had difficulty finding the Milford family. As a minister,
Reverend Milford had to move from place to place and was
now living below Dixons Mills, which was farther than I could
go on that visit. But I did see Minnie and Cluster, still doing

This picture was made more than sixty years after I taught at the little schoolhouse. Shortly afterward, the schoolhouse collapsed.

quite well on their small farm. They now had two children both healthy and pretty. They told me news about the other children. Cammie and Lily had both finished high school and each had jobs, saving money, they said, to attend the junior college.

One summer day I was sitting on our lawn swing when a car pulled into our drive and a tall, well-dressed young woman got out. She smiled and walked across the lawn to me. There was something very familiar about her walk and the tilt of her head. But I could not quite place her until she said "Hello, Miss Susie." Then I knew! It was Dimmie Milford. We hugged, and her face lit up with a smile.

"Dimmie," I said, "I am so glad to see you. Do sit down and tell me all about what you are doing. Minnie tells me you are a teacher now—what you always said you wanted to be. Are you happy with it?"

"Oh, I love it. And next year I'll get a promotion with a raise in salary. Then I can help the other girls go on with their educations. And maybe I can help Mother and Dad buy the little farm they want."

"Dimmie," I said, giving her another hug, "I am so proud of you," and I was. No one knew better than I what difficulties she had to face in getting her education.

We had a long and wonderful visit. When we said good-bye and she drove away, I sat back with a sigh of relief and reflected on the past.

When I took that job teaching, I was afraid I was too young and inexperienced, and I was. But seeing what these children who had so little had done with their lives, I felt that surely I must have given them something. As I reflected on the outcome, I came to feel that perhaps teaching that year in the little school in the cotton patch was the most worthwhile thing I had ever done.

About the Author

Susie Powers Tompkins, writer and award-winning artist, received her bachelor's degree from Alabama College, Montevallo, in 1928. Later she and her husband moved to Tuscaloosa where she owned a private school for speech and art for a number of years until World War II. During the war and the resulting teacher shortage, she began teaching first grade at Verner School. She taught there for more than fifteen years while raising her two children. Mrs. Tompkins still resides in Tuscaloosa and continues her artwork and writing.